Dr Amanda Brown is a GP at the largest women-only prison in Europe, Bronzefield. She was a regular NHS GP for a number of years, until she gave up her practice to move into the prison service. She worked at a teenage detention centre, before moving on to Wormwood Scrubs and then finally to Bronzefield where she continues to practise to this day.

D1392070

Also by Dr Amanda Brown

The Prison Doctor

THE

PRISON

DOCTOR:
WOMEN INSIDE

Stories from my time inside Britain's
biggest women's prison

DR AMANDA BROWN
WITH GEORGINA RODGERS

ONE PLACE. MANY STORIES

HQ
An imprint of HarperCollins*Publishers* Ltd.
1 London Bridge Street
London SE1 9GF

This edition 2020

1
First published in Great Britain by
HQ, an imprint of HarperCollins*Publishers* Ltd. 2020

ISBN: 978-0-00-838573-6

This book is set in 11.3/16 pt. Sabon
Typeset by Type-it As, Norway

Printed and bound by
CPI Group, Croydon CR0 4YY

This is a work of non-fiction, based on real events. Names
and identifying characteristics and details have been changed
to protect the identity and privacy of individuals.

This book deals with sexual assault, substance abuse and other
difficult topics. The author has taken great lengths to ensure the
subject matter is dealt with in a compassionate and respectful way,
but it may be troubling for some readers. Discretion is advised.

In loving memory always of my beloved mother and father, and of their unconditional love and the values they instilled in me.

'But there is that within me which will tire torture and time, and breathe when I expire.'
LORD BYRON

'Out beyond ideas of wrongdoing and rightdoing, there is a field. I'll meet you there.'

RUMI

This book is dedicated to all the abused and homeless women I have met at Bronzefield, and to so many other fascinating people who have been kind enough to share their stories with me, with gratitude, love and respect.

Chapter One

**'I've got no one and nothing,
not even my own teeth'**

MURDER

The word sprung out at me from the smudged screen of the computer and my heart sank. I was in my small and windowless consulting room in Bronzefield prison. I was halfway through an evening Reception shift, meeting new prisoners to assess and discuss their medical issues and prescribe any medication they might need. I was only two hours into my shift but was already feeling weary. Despite having met many prisoners who had committed murder, the impact of the word always caused the same reaction in me: shock, horror, and a deep sadness.

I scrolled up the screen to read the nurse's entry.

Rebecca was 27 years old and it was her first time in prison. That in itself was a surprise. I have seen so many prisoners return time and time again, that when I meet someone who has never been inside before, it's unusual.

Many of the residents' lives are so chaotic, complex and traumatic, that for some of them prison is a refuge. A shelter for the homeless and often a place to get help with addictions. The women return for a variety of crimes, such as shoplifting, theft, robbery, burglary, fraud, arson, kidnap, GBH or ABH.

Rarely murder.

*

When I reached the holding cell, I saw the door was open and there were five women in there. Two were lying down on the stark blue plastic bench seating, looking extremely unwell, most probably because they were withdrawing from drugs. One was pale and sweaty, her hair sticking to her forehead and her eyes shut, as she tried to ride it out. The other was clutching her stomach, groaning miserably – not an unfamiliar sound to me. An overweight woman in a wheelchair stared blankly ahead of her. The other two sat quietly, and appeared to be shaken and fearful.

'Rebecca?' I asked as I looked around the room.

A girl's eyes peered out from her curtain of long, deep brown hair like a cornered animal. She looked much younger than her age, with delicate features, a spray of freckles and intense eyes. She was wearing a knee-length skirt with tights and pale pink pumps, which were splattered with something dark, as was her pale grey top. I tried not to show the shock and surprise I felt, as I realised it was blood. She must have come straight to prison from the scene of the crime.

I led her back along the mottled-blue lino floor of the corridor to my room.

'Hi, Rebecca. I'm Doctor Brown. Come and have a seat.' I gestured to the hard and battered plastic chair. 'I just have to go through some routine questions to make sure you are okay and see if you need any medication,' I told her. 'Alright?'

She didn't reply.

I started to go through her notes. She looked shocked to her core. Her hands were trembling, and she fiddled with her cuffs, pulling them over her hands. I noticed that they were also stained dark and dirty with dried blood. I could smell it.

Metallic. Slightly sweet.

Rebecca's eyes looked glazed and vacant; the look of someone who could not believe where she was or what was happening to her.

'I can see here that you are charged with murder,' I said. 'Can you tell me what happened?'

'I killed my partner.' Her voice was clear but started to crack as she said the word 'partner'.

I could see she was trying hard to stop the tears, which were pricking the corners of her eyes, from falling. She swallowed hard.

'I stabbed him.' She looked up at me through her fringe. 'I just couldn't take it any more. I couldn't see a way out. The years of being controlled.' She grimaced, and her voice became more defiant. 'I was his punch bag. I just couldn't do it any more.'

I was already fairly sure what she was going to say, having heard it so many times in Bronzefield before.

She rolled into her story, the floodgates opening. Sitting in front of me was a criminal, charged with the most serious of crimes, but she was just a normal person. She was well spoken, intelligent and articulate. She reminded me a little of the girl who cuts my hair.

Rebecca met her partner when she was 15 and he was 21. For a while, she said, they were just friends. When she was 17, he persuaded her that they would be better as a couple than as friends.

'It sounds like such a cliché now, but he did everything for me,' she said, her eyes downcast. 'He treated me like a queen. He drove me to college, helped with my work, there was nothing he wouldn't do for me. Everyone thought he was great; me, my parents, my friends. He was literally the golden guy. My mates really thought I'd lucked out.'

I nodded. 'When did things change?'

'It went wrong the first time we went away together. We went on holiday to Spain after I finished my A levels,' she said. 'He planned and paid for everything, said it was his way of celebrating the end of my exams. While we were there, he saw me talking to a man. I can't even remember who he was now; a waiter, I think. We were just talking and laughing; it was completely innocent.

'That was the first time he hit me.

'He accused me of flirting. I had nowhere to go, so I stayed in the hotel room, cowering in the bathroom.'

I could see a flash of fear in her eyes as she recalled what had happened.

'The next day, he was so apologetic. He was sobbing. He said he would kill himself if I left him. I'd never seen him cry like that. It was impossible not to forgive him. I covered up the bruises on my face with make-up and wore a sarong all holiday. I didn't even go swimming in the hotel pool. I just sat on a sunbed, hugging my bruised ribs. God, it hurt so much that time.

'That was just the start.'

It was a story that I had heard countless times before. The details and cast were different, of course, but the story of domestic abuse and violence is all too familiar. Men trying to control women and, so often, going too far.

Rebecca's partner dominated her.

'Then, of course, he persuaded me to not take the place I got at university – it was over two hours away from where we lived. He made me move in with him. He cut me off from my friends and family and monitored my every move.

'He made me think I was in the wrong. Always. My attitude was wrong, my clothes were wrong, I looked like a slut,' she explained.

I could hear the hurt and anger in her voice as she spoke. I knew that women like Rebecca often became increasingly intimidated, and frenzied with fear about when the next blow was coming, so they did everything they could to keep the peace.

'When one of my colleagues at my office job told me I'd

had "one bruise too many", and asked me if I needed to talk, I felt I had no choice but to resign. I never went back to work. I even stopped going to see my GP in case they suspected him. He called home throughout the day to check up on me. I felt suffocated.'

Rebecca's partner worked as an accountant and they lived in a nice part of Surrey, not that far away from the prison, with their five-year-old son.

'So, what happened today?' I asked gently.

'I was in the kitchen. I was making his lunch. He always has it at 1 p.m. on the dot – he leaves the office to come home to check on me. I could see he was in one of his moods. He gets kind of twitchy, you know?'

I didn't correct her tense.

'He mentioned Jack. He's not long been at school, and he's had a few scuffles already in the playground. Just typical five-year-old boy stuff – a bit of pushing and shoving, nothing really. He said he wants him to be a man, like him. We started to row – about Jack, about everything. I hate the fact I'm stuck at home all day. All I do is clean the house. He won't let me go anywhere or do anything. I even have to ask his permission to go to the shop to buy a pint of milk. I feel so lonely. So alone. All the time. Apart from Jack – he means everything to me. He gives me purpose… '

She tailed off, deep in thought, her face slightly brighter as she spoke about her son.

'I can tell Jack knows what goes on. He always wets the bed when we've had a fight. He knows what his dad's like; it's all he's ever known. Heavy fists and muffled sobs.' Rebecca's hair fell in front of her eyes and she pushed it away, then rested her head in one hand.

'I couldn't let him hurt my son like he hurts me. I just lost it, I... I'd been making sandwiches and the bread knife was on the surface, and the carving knife. I just grabbed the carving knife and stabbed him. I didn't honestly realise what was happening until it was too late.'

It struck me how desperate Rebecca must have been to do something like that. How powerful that feeling of hopelessness and despair must've been for her to physically do that to him,

To strike him hard enough to kill him.

'The only time he ever stopped hitting me was when I was pregnant. But once Jack arrived, he started again, saying I was putting the baby before him. Always seeing to Jack and never looking after him. There were so many times he almost killed me. Believe me. It was either us or him.

'I got him in the chest. There was blood everywhere. I couldn't quite believe I'd done it. I've never hurt a fly. He staggered around for a minute or two, shouting at me, and then fell on the floor.' Rebecca's voice was dull and unemotional as she relayed what had happened. Her eyes were glassy and her face was expressionless. I imagined the true horror of the event would not sink in for many days, or even weeks or months.

'I still couldn't believe what I'd done. It was like I was in a dream that I couldn't wake up from. The blood was spreading all over the floor, and he lay there completely still. I was panicking, but knew I had to do the right thing. I called the police and then my mum. Before I knew it, two paramedics arrived. The police must have sent them. They said he was still alive. They tried to save him, but he died within minutes of them turning up.

'I wanted to clean up the kitchen. I got the mop out. I didn't want to leave it for someone else to do, but the police wouldn't let me. They brought me straight here.'

Rightly or wrongly, I felt for her. I could see she didn't realise the enormity of what she had done. She was desperate, and like so many of the women I see, was despairing and couldn't see a way out.

*

We continued to go through Rebecca's notes. She didn't use drugs and was not a heavy drinker and she had no medical issues. She was a young woman, who was fit and well.

'What am I going to do about my son? Will I see him?' Her voice sounded almost hopeful, that things would not change for her and her son.

For most mothers, being apart from their children must cause the most indescribable pain. I simply couldn't imagine what that must be like for anyone, especially for someone with very young children.

'You said your mum's got him?' I replied, softly.

'Yes. She said she would pick him up from school. I guess

he must've had his tea by now. Done his reading – he's starting to read now. It's amazing, and the books are so funny. He'll be in bed by now, I suppose. I hope he has his favourite teddy.' She paused, her mind ticking over, like most mothers, the things they do every night to keep their kids happy and comfortable. 'When will I see him again?'

'I'm sorry. I don't know,' I replied. All I did know was that the chances were, if she was found guilty to the charge of murder, she was likely to be in prison for a very long time.

I put my hand gently on hers. 'I can't imagine how you must be feeling. I hope you cope with being in prison, and that you will soon be able to see your little boy.'

The prison officer standing outside came in and led her away. That was the first and last time I ever saw Rebecca. I never knew whether she lived to regret what she had done, or if she was able to see her son regularly whilst she was inside. I simply got a snapshot of her existence, and happened to be there on what must have been the most shocking and tragic day of her life.

*

The Reception shift in Bronzefield involved seeing to the new prisoners who had arrived from one of the ninety-five courts the prison serves, or from police custody, before they were taken to the house blocks by the officers to start their stint behind bars. Many of them would be withdrawing from a medley of drugs and alcohol, and would need medication to get them through the night. My shift started at 5 p.m. and lasted until 9 p.m. but it was often not possible to see all the new arrivals in that time. They would be seen by the on-call doctor, if needs be. Whatever crimes they had committed, they still needed to be cared for. Some had very complex physical and mental health issues, arriving with bags of different medications: a jumble of boxes, bottles and pill packets, some of them empty, often many of them out of date. Sometimes it seemed to me like they had simply swept the top of their bedside table into a bag in anticipation of not going home for a while. These medications needed to be checked and prescribed on the computer, before the nurses could administer them.

I felt pensive after seeing Rebecca, and wondered how she would cope with the days that would follow, away from her son. I took a deep breath of stuffy air and padded out of my room, along the strip-lit hallway to the small waiting area.

A warming smell of jacket potatoes wafted out of the little kitchen area and made my stomach rumble, reminding me of the fact I hadn't eaten since mid-morning. Food is provided in Reception for the new arrivals who won't make it back to the house block in time for the evening meal. The kitchen is kitted out with a small fridge, microwave and chest freezer, supplying the basics, including bread for toast. Often dinner for the new arrivals is a simple jacket potato, with a dollop of beans and handful of cheese.

It was obviously a jacket potato day. For many of them, it would be their first proper cooked meal in days.

*

'Hi, Doc.' Melissa and Shamir, two prison officers, greeted me, smiling. We exchanged a few words.

'It's really busy tonight,' Melissa said with a sigh. She sounded exasperated as she tried to sort out one of the girl's possessions – a jumble of clothing and prescription medicine that she was passing over the large countertop. Behind the wide counter are rows upon rows of small lockers to house the women's possessions whilst they are inside. When they are released, they are given back the items.

'Yes, it looks crazy,' I replied, scanning the scene in front of me.

The process of getting into the prison can be slow. Some cases are more complex than others. After prisoners arrive inside from their ride in the uncomfortable 'sweat box' to the prison, they are processed into the system. This involves searches, sorting their clothing, and getting their 'welcome pack'.

I could see one girl being handed a white string bag, containing a handful of items, including a mug, a plastic knife, fork and spoon, toothpaste, toothbrush, shampoo, soap, conditioner, six pairs of knickers and socks, two tracksuits, a nightie, tea and coffee, and a hairbrush. These packs are compiled by the residents who work in Reception, earning from £2.40 to £3.20 a day, which they can spend how they wish on items like moisturiser, vapes and snacks. The girls can also take some of their own clothes to wear, if they wish, but many of them only have the clothes that they are standing up in. The prisoners then meet with the nurse, to go through their medical notes, and all those that require medication would be added to my list. There could sometimes be more than fifteen new residents needing to be processed, and sometimes I would need to spend thirty to forty minutes going through their medical history and medication. Any newcomer that had not been seen by the end of my shift would be seen by the duty doctor for any essential medication and then added to the GP list to be reviewed the following morning. It was a finely tuned process that was often exhausting and challenging. But at times, it was also very rewarding. It kept me on my toes, and it was definitely never boring.

*

There were women standing and sitting everywhere, up and down the corridor. The noise was bouncing off the walls.

One woman was screaming to the officer: 'But I don't wanna share a fucking cell. Last time I was in 'ere I was put in with a right wrong 'un. I ain't sharing again. I got to 'ave a single cell.'

There were also happy shrieks and joyful whoops as girls were reunited with familiar faces from previous sentences. Also in the mix were a handful of girls who looked withdrawn, scared and bedraggled.

Some women were heading off to have a shower,

clutching thin towels and small bottles of shower gel. There are showers within the Reception area along the main corridor, so once the women have checked their belongings in, many choose to have a wash, especially those who are homeless and may not have showered for days. Others were on the two phones, chatting noisily to their families and recounting the events of the day, whilst some girls queued patiently behind them, obviously desperate to speak with their families before they got locked up for the night. Several were walking to the toilets with small plastic pots, to provide urine samples, screening for infection, drugs, and if indicated, pregnancy.

Also milling up and down the corridor were peer support workers in blue T-shirts.

These are longer-term residents who help new arrivals find their feet and answer the many questions they may have about prison life. During their first few days in prison, residents are said to be at their most vulnerable, and are at high risk of self-harm. I smiled at one of the peer support workers, Amber, as I passed her. Petite, with dark features, she was always positive and upbeat. We often worked together in Reception and I loved her bright and warm company. She gave me a cheerful nod back as she guided a new arrival to one of the small interview rooms. Through the cacophony of noise, I could easily hear her talking with reassuring and soothing tones. This peer support can be invaluable in helping the women through the first few hours.

Some women were waiting in small holding areas to see

the nurse or to go through paperwork. As I walked along, I could see another woman locked in a holding room, shouting at the top of her voice to be let out, and banging the door with her shoe, her dreadlocked hair sticking out in all directions and her eyes wild.

The noise ricocheted around me as the throbbing life of prison Reception played out its daily drama.

*

Scrolling down my list, I spotted a familiar name. Shannon was someone I'd grown to know well. Repeat offenders, sometimes called the 'frequent flyers' by prison staff, make up by far the majority of the women I meet. So much so that one of the questions on the medical template I go through when I see them is to ask when they were last released from prison. When Shannon came back into custody I was never surprised because she had been homeless for years. I was always glad to see her as I had grown to like and understand her. It was like meeting an old friend again and made my job so much more enjoyable. But every time she was released, I hoped I wouldn't see her back again.

I looked into the waiting area and saw her sitting down with her head in her hands. Rather than jump up and greet me with her usual toothless grin and a 'Hello, Doc!' I could see she was agitated and crying. She was wearing a grubby blue tracksuit. I glimpsed the top of her head; her auburn hair was matted and greasy.

'Shannon?'

She looked up and slumped back in her chair for a moment, a look of relief on her haggard and pock-marked face.

'Come on,' I said as I led her to my little room.

I shut the door and she gave me a hug as the various smells associated with living rough, like body odour, dirty feet, and foul breath, soon filled the air.

'What's happened? You're never normally like this?' I asked.

'Doc… it's good to see you. The judge… he said…' She started sobbing. Messy and loud, snot-filled sobs. 'He called me a worthless wretch.'

A worthless wretch, I thought, *what an awful thing to say.*

I was momentarily stunned by the language the judge had used. Judges can use their summary judgements to say what they like and whilst this is normally a standard administrative process, this judge had obviously made his personal views known. I couldn't help but think about the vast gulf between the day-to-day lives of Shannon and the judge who had just sentenced her. Society and the judge might see Shannon as a useless criminal, but she didn't see herself like that, and neither did I, because I understood the dreadful details of her life that inevitably had led Shannon to commit crime.

'You are not worthless, and you are not a wretch,' I told her firmly. 'I really believe you can make something of your life. And I am sure you will, if you can get the help you need.'

I tore off a large piece of paper towel from the roll and passed it to her. She clutched it and wiped her dirty face. Shannon had substance misuse issues and I could already see the signs of withdrawal. Beads of sweat were visible on her forehead and she had goosebumps on her track-marked arms.

We started to go through the routine medical questions, though I knew Shannon's medical history well. After all, this was the ninth time I had seen her in around two years.

'Okay, let's sort out your medication Shannon, so that you can go over to House Block One as soon as possible to get your methadone,' I said.

*

Before my time in prison I had worked as a GP for twenty years in the community near where I live in Buckinghamshire, but had very rarely treated patients who had ever been involved with the criminal justice system. Like many others, the mainstream media soundbites meant that before I started to work in prisons, my opinion was condensed down into a narrative of 'good people' and 'bad people', with a clichéd list of 'bad' characters ranging from violent psychopath to petty criminal. The reality is far more complex.

Female offenders are some of the most vulnerable people within our society. Women make up just five per cent of the prison population in England and Wales, and the vast majority are imprisoned for non-violent offences, and are often sentenced for a matter of just weeks at a time. Many of them are caught in a vicious cycle of domestic violence, drug abuse and homelessness. Written off by society, they disappear into a world that most of us are oblivious to, of lost invisible souls who have no voice. I am now all too aware of the awful lives so many of them have to endure, as are many other people and organisations who work tirelessly to try to help in all sorts of different ways.

These are often brave, funny and kind women, who are trapped, and without hope so often of a better life, and they are at risk of being dismissed and vilified by society. They are human like us, and they face the same battles many of us do, yet their lives are just much harder.

There are many, many issues and obstacles in the way of them rehabilitating and breaking free of the way of life they are caught up in. Their lives are often desperate and can spiral into the most savage circumstances. Far too many of them are sleeping on the streets. If they are lucky, they may 'sofa-surf' with friends and family, but all too often they inevitably head back to the streets, having outstayed their invitation. The last time I had seen Shannon, she had been sleeping in a stairwell near Victoria station. She'd told me the day before her release that she was planning to return to her old spot and had given me a scrappy piece of paper with biro scrawl, which read 'Elizabeth Bridge, Victoria.'

'Come and try and find me, won't you? When you're next in London,' she'd said, like any old friend inviting me round for a coffee. I wanted Shannon to hope for a better life for herself, however impossible it may seem given the shocking life she was living on the streets. In reality, her life was one of despair and hopelessness. Despair was sadly evident in so many of the people I had come to know through the course of my day-to-day work.

By far the majority of the women I see have experienced or continue to experience some kind of trauma. Many have a history of domestic violence and sexual abuse. They live in terror and this leads to substance abuse, self-harm, suicide attempts and serious mental health issues.

'What are you in for this time?' I asked her gently.

'I nicked a laptop from Currys. Thought I could sell it to my mate, Mike – he's always got cash.'

'How long are you here for?'

'Just twenty-eight days. I was only out two weeks ago.'

Women often serve far shorter sentences for minor crimes like theft and shoplifting and are locked up for a matter of weeks, before leaving to go back onto the streets, only to reoffend and come back in – hence the frequent flyer moniker. The longest sentence Shannon had received was two years when she was in her late teens.

She was now 26 and had been using drugs for over a decade.

'How much heroin are using at the moment, Shannon?' I asked. 'Are you still buying benzos and pregabs as well?'

'I usually spend about 100 quid on crack and a 100 quid on heroin every day,' she told me. 'I'm also taking about 40mg of diazepam and as many pregabs as I can get my hands on. The drugs and booze just get me through. Some days I feel like I'm drowning. It all just helps me to forget the evil shit I've been through.'

'How much are you drinking now?' I asked.

'A bottle of vodka a day, if I can get it,' she replied staring at her feet.

Shannon sat forward, grasping her stomach and wincing in pain because she had really bad abdominal cramps due to withdrawal.

'I think I'm gonna be sick,' she said, clutching her hand to her mouth.

I looked around the room for a disposable bowl and fortunately found one in the corner, which I quickly handed to her.

'Here you go, Shannon,' I said.

I sat and waited in silence until she felt able to continue talking.

'I live from one hit to the next. I owe my dealers money and I spend my life in fear. They keep coming after me. Say I owe them more and more. I've lost track of it all now, and I don't know how I'm going to pay them back.' She sounded terrified. Women were not simply scared of violent partners. Men dominating these women came in all guises. Many women turn to sex work to keep their dealers happy.

She had also been sleeping rough for the majority of her adult life, heading to the streets with a measly bag of possessions and a sleeping bag to find somewhere she could call her own – even if this was a shop door, in a stairwell or under a bridge. Solving housing issues for this section of society is hugely challenging. Many organisations use online systems to process requests and details, but women without their own phone or access to the internet cannot get near them. Shannon always sold the cheap phones she got her hands on for drugs, and aside from the odd night in a hostel, she was on her own. She had no bank account. She had fallen through all the nets.

Over the many hours I had spent before then with Shannon trying to tackle her drug and alcohol dependency, I had heard her story in full.

'My dad beat up my mum so badly when she was expecting me, it's a miracle I'm here at all,' she said. 'Even after all that, she stayed with him. He was locked up when I was two and I never saw him again.'

Her mum worked three jobs to put food on the table and became involved with another man. Her new stepfather soon moved into the house.

'He was a bastard. Mum had two more kids with him. He would play us all off against each other. It was like some sort of weird power game of cat and mouse.'

Her face looked pale and impassive.

'We would all be beaten in turn. I was always the last because I'm the eldest. Listening to my sisters cry and scream before me was unbearable.' Her voice started to crack.

'I would hide under my duvet and put my pillow over my head, but nothing would drown out the noise.'

The tears started to fall as she relived the memory. I gently placed my hand on her arm, a little comfort as she talked.

'My stepdad would beat and rape my mum in front of us, and he would come into our rooms after Mum left at night. She worked as a cleaner at the local leisure centre.'

'He sounds like a really evil man,' I said, deeply sickened by her awful tale.

'First, it was just weird touching, but when I was eight, he started raping me. I could never scream, as he was so heavy. I felt I couldn't breathe. I would just look at the tree outside my window and pray it would be over,' she told me. 'I never told my mum. I didn't want her to be upset.' The lengths people would go to protect the people they loved never ceased to amaze me, and often left me speechless. I frequently met people who took the blame for crimes they did not commit; from mothers who claimed the drugs in the house were theirs and not their kid's, to girlfriends who provided an alibi or who covered up for their partners in other ways.

'Me and my sisters were always hungry, and I sometimes passed out at school. I was terrified about my mum getting into trouble, so I would lie and say that I'd had some toast or cereal for breakfast.'

Thankfully, Shannon's mum met someone new and their lives changed for a few years. The abuse stopped and there was more money for food, and birthday and Christmas presents.

When Shannon met her first boyfriend at 14, sadly the cycle of abuse started again. She became dependent on drugs and alcohol and started bunking off school. Her grades had never been good, and she was struggling to keep up. Eventually, her mum threw her out, because she didn't want her drug use to influence her sisters. She ended up on the streets. She had no qualifications, and having lost contact with her mum and sisters a long time ago, she also had no support network on the outside.

'I've got no one and nothing. Not even my own teeth,' she said, showing me a gappy mouth with a few rotten, brown teeth, worn down to stumps from the years of drug use and neglect.

Those words seemed to sum up the story of so many women I had come to know during my time working at Bronzefield.

I knew Shannon's history and needed to help her manage the symptoms of alcohol withdrawal, and to stabilise her on methadone whilst she was in prison. Realistically there was not enough time for her to detox from methadone, and there was also a risk of her overdosing on heroin after release if she was on too low a dose. It was not going to be easy for her; it never was.

I had learnt early on in my time at Bronzefield that the women themselves had to want to stop using drugs and conquer their addictions. No matter what I or anybody else did or said, it was up to them to make that choice and see it through.

'I haven't got any drugs in my lady pocket, Doctor Brown. Honest,' she said. I knew that she had smuggled drugs into prison in her vagina before – it was an obvious way for many prisoners, as internal searches are not permitted.

She looked up and gave me a smile, so I would know. If she told me she had drugs on her I would have to report her, so I swiftly moved on to sorting out her medication. As we chatted away, the upset of the judge's comments seemed to fade, and I started to see the old smiley Shannon emerge.

'To be honest, in some ways I'm happy to be back and have a warm place to sleep. It's getting proper cold out there now. My sleeping bag got soaked in the rain the other night and it just won't dry. And I'm starving,' she rattled on. 'I can't just sit there all day. Shoplifting gives me something to do. That, and riding round the Circle Line. It's warm, and much more comfortable than just sitting on the street. I also feel safer when I'm not sitting on the street. I'm so scared the dealers will find me and beat me up again.

'It'll be nice to be with some of my mates again. We understand each other. I'll keep busy in here, maybe try and learn something; get back on the education programme. It's good to know I'll feel safe at night again, for a while.'

This was something I heard again and again from the prisoners. Being in prison for many women is far safer than being on the outside. She was back in a place she associated with safety, familiarity, security, and even opportunity. With three meals a day and regimented timetabling, she also wouldn't need to make many decisions for herself.

As well as addictions to crack cocaine – a crystallised form of cocaine – and heroin, Shannon drank heavily and was addicted to benzodiazepines and pregabalin. Highly addictive, benzodiazepines – referred to as 'benzos' by the inmates – are drugs like diazepam and Xanax and were originally prescribed for anxiety when they first came on the market in the 1960s. Many girls I see are addicted to high doses of these drugs because it calms them down. Pregabalin is another prescription-only drug used to treat epilepsy, general anxiety disorder and neuropathic pain. Like heroin, it induces feelings of euphoria and calmness and is hugely addictive, so there is a rampant black market for this drug. Many of the women I see say that it is harder to withdraw from pregabalin than heroin.

'It's just so awful,' they tell me, with haunted expressions.

Shannon was addicted to so much that withdrawal from it all was medically a blurred picture. Her face was glistening with sweat and her hands were shaking. As she looked at me, I could see that her pupils were widely dilated. She would experience a whole range of debilitating symptoms over the coming days and possibly weeks, including diarrhoea, abdominal cramps, nausea and vomiting, shivering, sweating, anxiety, panic attacks and paranoia.

I started typing out a whole list of medications that she would need to enable her to cope.

Methadone is prescribed as a substitute for heroin and helps to ease withdrawal symptoms from opiates and reduce the cravings. Bright green in colour, it is a slow-acting opiate substitute and is prescribed in a liquid form. Most people that take it say that it tastes disgusting. In the past, all prisoners were expected to detox completely from methadone if they were due to remain in custody for more than three months, but this is no longer the case. Often, especially in the case of a short sentence, it has to be 'titrated up', to try to protect the user from overdosing on release, or to control their dreadful symptoms of withdrawal.

Prisoners are given their daily dose by the nurses at 9 a.m. but if the dose is not high enough, it won't hold them through until the next day.

We agreed on a dose to build up to, and along with methadone, I prescribed all the other medications she would need to combat her withdrawal symptoms.

'I know I say this every time I see you,' Shannon grinned. 'But you really are like a mother to me. Thank you.'

I stood up to give her another hug.

'Good luck, Shannon,' I told her. 'Be good.'

'I'll try, I really will.'

Deep down, I knew I would almost certainly be seeing her again after her current stay. I always, always hoped girls like Shannon would get their lives back on track, but it felt like she had the odds stacked against her. The statistics state that the more previous custodial sentences a woman has had, the higher her reoffending rate; the reoffending rate for women with eleven or more previous convictions is eighty-three per cent. It's sad but it makes sense that just as women's paths into crime are chaotic and complex, so their paths out to a better life are likely to hit just as many bumps along the road.

*

I glanced at my watch. It was just past 8 p.m. and I was feeling really tired and ready to go home. Despite the fact that I had been working in prisons for many years, I had never become immune to the rawness of it; the shock, fear, relief, sadness, shame, despair. It was a melting pot of extremes, and emotionally draining. So often, I was all too aware that I had very little to offer the people I was meeting, as I could not change the fact of where they were and what they had done. All I could hope to do was to try and offer a bit of kindness and reassurance, and to relieve any physical pain and suffering they may be going through. I try my best, if I possibly can, to take the edge off their undoubted apprehension, as I realise it must be so overwhelming and intimidating for some people to find themselves in prison. It is strange that whatever their crime and however awful, it fades into the background momentarily and I just see them as a scared and shocked human being. I am so used to the environment that I feel totally comfortable within the prison walls. But I find myself trying to imagine seeing it through their eyes, and wonder how it would feel if I was sitting in that chair opposite me.

As I was finishing off my notes on Shannon, Amber popped in to ask if I would like a cup of coffee.

'I would love one. Thank you, Amber,' I replied without giving it a second thought. 'How has your day been? Any gossip?' I asked her, hoping for a little light relief. Amber always cheered me up, as she is blessed with such a wonderful sunny nature and positive outlook on life.

'Nothing much, Doctor Brown,' she replied. 'Same old, same old. I'm really happy though, because my family are coming to visit tomorrow, and I can't wait to see them. Also, I'm reading a brilliant book – a thriller – which is really gripping.'

We chatted for a few minutes about the book and then she went off to get me a drink. It felt good to have people like Amber around. During my time working in Reception, I had become very close with the women who worked there and we tried to look out for each other. I thought how lucky I was to have them with me; we were like a little family and there was a lovely sense of belonging between us. Whenever I felt a bit down, they always managed to cheer me up.

A prison officer wheeled the next patient along the corridor, manoeuvring the heavy chair with some difficulty, taking a number of turns to get into my room.

In front of me was a black woman, in clean clothes and bright mauve lipstick. She was very overweight, with rolls of flesh sagging over the side of her chair.

I glanced at her notes. Gloria was 68 and had a multitude

of medical complaints, including a condition that affected her joints. I read that she had already undergone two hip replacements. She also suffered from type 2 diabetes and hypertension, and was unable to walk due to the severe pain in her knees. This explained the wheelchair.

'Hi Gloria, I'm Doctor Brown...' I started telling her about what I was doing and why she had been sent to see me.

I went through my usual questions, one of which was to ask what she had been charged with.

Gloria explained that she had been charged with fraud, but she denied any involvement.

'... but I didn't do it,' she said. 'I got caught up in something I didn't understand. I didn't realise it was illegal. I've been given three years, Doctor Brown. Three years! Surely that's not right?' She looked at me imploringly. 'I've never been in trouble before in my life.'

Gloria had come straight from the court where she had been sentenced, so it was clear that whatever she felt, the judge felt differently.

Fraud is not an uncommon crime, and includes benefit fraud and other far more elaborate types of fraud, including complex money laundering. This is one of the convictions that many women really struggle to come terms with. They often feel angry that they have ended up in prison as they didn't realise the severity of what they were doing.

I asked her about her long and complicated medical history. As we chatted it was clear that Gloria's main support was from her husband, Reg. They lived north of Manchester on their own and didn't have children. They only had each other.

'It's not going to be easy for him to come and see me, is it?' she said, looking despondent

'When you get to the house block, have a chat with the officers,' I told her. 'They'll be able to help you, and tell you what you need to do next to try and arrange a visit.'

I knew the prison did their best to help residents maintain family ties by facilitating visits and contact, but of course, as with most things in life, there are forms to fill and protocols to follow.

'Who's going to help me get in and out of bed?' she asked. 'Reg does that for me. He gets me up, cooks my breakfast and helps me get dressed. He sits me in front of *This Morning* on the TV, before he goes to get the paper.

'I'll be lost without him,' she continued. 'I just don't know how I'm going to cope.'

She continued to tell me about their daily routine, down to the finest detail, with Reg featuring in every element of her day. I felt for Gloria. Her sentence was years, not months, and it was going to be hard for her to adjust, assuming she ever would.

Thirty minutes later, I had completed her notes on the computer and prescribed everything she would need for the time being. She looked relieved but nervous.

'They will get my pills to me on time, won't they?' she

asked, her eyes flicking from me to the computer and back again.

For many women, the fact they are not allowed to keep their medication with them, that it is handed out by the nurses, is another loss of liberty.

'The nurses will give your medication to you each day,' I explained. 'Once you are settled, you will have an in-possession risk assessment – it's called an IPRA – to see if you can look after your own medication. But up until then, I'm afraid you'll just have to go to the nurses for it.'

She looked resigned to the fact that there was nothing she could say to alter the situation.

She added: 'The other thing is I also suffer from claus-trophobia. I hate being in lifts, and any small space, in fact. Even being in this room makes me feel nervous.'

Gloria's new home would be a small cell, with only enough space for a narrow bed, sink, desk and a toilet. With a door that would be locked. And many doors would be locked behind that door.

As I finished my shift that evening and walked across the car park to make my way home around the M25, I wondered how Gloria, Rebecca and Shannon, and the other women I had met that night, would cope with the new phase of their lives. How prepared they would be for the many challenges they might face, and how they would handle them.

Chapter Two

**'I know I am being punished but I don't
want my child to be punished too'**

'Just look at his tiny fingers.'

I was sitting in the little consulting room in the Healthcare wing one morning during my regular clinic. In front of me was a new mother gazing into her buggy. Inside the buggy was the most beautiful baby, his face all scrunched up, his fists clenched and hot cheeks glowing. His eyes twitched and opened momentarily like he was having the most vivid and exhilarating dream. At four weeks old, the smattering of milk spots on his nose, cheeks and forehead, a common and completely normal skin condition that babies get, were starting to fade. Megan had tucked him in carefully, with a soft grey blanket decorated with ducks, covering him to his chest. On his head, he was wearing a knitted blue hat.

'He's gorgeous, Megan. I'm really happy for you.' I smiled at her. 'Congratulations.'

'I never thought I could love something as much as I love him,' she continued, looking tenderly at him. 'Dylan has made me want to be a better person, to do better, y'know?'

I nodded.

As a mother, of course I knew. There is something about having children that makes most people determined to be the best versions of themselves they can possibly be.

My regular GP clinic at Bronzefield does not discriminate. In addition to dealing with lots of drug and alcohol issues, patients arrive with a whole selection of medical complaints, some more serious than others. From time to time, this includes new mothers, who enter my clinic with their little charges in tow. They are just like any other mothers of newborns outside prison: usually exhausted and often with grey shadows under their eyes, sometimes pale and feeling sore after the birth, but more often than not, completely in love with their babies.

She brushed her hand through her cropped, dyed red hair and gazed lovingly at her son.

'I do feel guilty he's been born while I'm in here,' she added. 'I don't want him to hate me for it when he's older. But I'm going to make it up to him. Do better. I know I'm being punished but I don't want him to be punished too. I'm trying to make the best of it.

'My room on the MBU is great, I love it there. I've made it really cosy and Dylan has his little corner with all his stuff. I never knew babies could get through so many nappies and clothes!'

Alongside the house blocks at Bronzefield is an established twelve-room Mother and Baby Unit (MBU). As well as rooms for single babies, there is one room specifically designed for mothers of twins, taking the child capacity to thirteen. This allows women who give birth while they are in prison to stay with their children until they are 18 months old.

Megan had moved to the unit as soon as she returned from hospital just after she had given birth.

'I was like a whale before Dylan was born, my bump got to a room five minutes before I did,' she laughed. 'I was enormous!'

'How was the birth?' I asked.

'I went by ambulance to the local hospital. It was a bit weird, having the officers there with me, but at least I didn't have to be cuffed to them. The rules have changed, apparently,' she said.

'They were outside the room and I was screaming and shouting so much I had a sore throat afterwards! They were nice though, and joked that their ears were ringing when it was all finally over.' She then smiled sadly. 'I could choose a birthing partner to be with me, and I'd have loved my mum to be with me, y'know, or my sister, but they live too far away.

'I can't wait for them to meet him at next month's Stay and Play Day at the MBU. Mum is absolutely desperate to meet him.

'The birth went on for hours. It was so painful, I thought I was gonna die,' she said, rhythmically pushing her buggy backwards and forwards in the tiny room. 'Honestly, it's a bit of a blur now. But he's okay, and that's all that matters, really, isn't it?'

'Of course it is, you've done really well... I hope you're managing to get as much rest as you can. It's so important,' I told her. 'So, how can I help you today, Megan?'

'It's my tits. They've both been a bit sore, but now the left one's red and feels rock hard and like it's on fire. It's really painful too!'

'Okay, let's have a look and see what's going on. Can you lie down on the couch and let me examine you?'

Megan lay down and then pulled up her Nike jumper and released her breasts from the greying nursing bra.

'The bra ain't very sexy – one of the other mums on the MBU gave it to me, but at least there's no one else to see it, thank goodness,' she laughed.

'Don't I count?' I smiled.

Her left breast was engorged, red, and felt hot to touch. Her nipple was also cracked and tender.

'It's agony when I feed him,' she explained. I popped the thermometer in her ear and took her temperature, which was slightly raised. It was clear that she had mastitis, an infection that occurs in the tissue of the breast, most commonly during breast-feeding.

'Are you still managing to breast-feed him?' I asked her.

'Yeah, all he wants to do all the time is feed, feed, feed. He's a right greedy guts!' she said. 'It took a while to get the hang of it, and my god, my tits were a mess at the start – but we got there in the end.'

'You look like you've been doing a brilliant job,' I told her. 'He is a really good size.'

She beamed at me with a wide smile, proud as punch. 'Yeah, he's put on 200 grams this week... I feel close to him when I feed him. Loads of the other girls don't wanna do it, say it messes up your body and going on formula is easier. But I'm gonna try to stick with it, at least while I can.'

'Good for you,' I said. Breast-feeding is an excellent way for new mums to bond with their babies and feel close to them, which is perhaps even more important when in prison than at home, where they would most likely be surrounded by friends and family.

Another of nature's powerful tools.

'Keep feeding him as much as you can,' I told her. 'It might help to ease the pain a bit. Just make sure he is properly attached.'

'He's going to the nursery in two weeks though,' Megan added. 'They've told me I need to go back to work. I'm doing a course in catering, which I love, and I'm really hoping I can open my own little business selling sandwiches in offices when I get out of here.'

'I hear wonderful things about the nursery,' I told her. Within the MBU, which is set apart from the main accommodation units, is an OFSTED-registered nursery, Little Stars, which allows the mums to do their prison jobs and education with the rest of the residents, whilst their babies are looked after by nursery nurses, from around the time the babies are six to eight weeks old. 'It's a lovely place,' I told her. 'Bright and airy with a wonderful range of colourful toys and games. There are cots for the babies to nap in and the doors open to a courtyard area, with lots of outdoor toys, like ride-ons and a little toddler climbing frame.'

'I know, the other girls rave about it. And I already feel like I know the staff there really well. They're always helping us out. I dunno what I'm gonna do about feeding him then,' she added. 'Guess he'll have to go on the bottle. I'm feeling so exhausted though. I don't know how I'm ever gonna get back to work.'

'You'll be fine,' I told her. 'I'm sure you will manage. You strike me as being very strong and determined.'

I thought back to when I first met Megan when she first arrived at Bronzefield. I was working in Reception that evening. She had been in a very controlling relationship for about three years. She had never been in prison before and was so scared and shocked, as she said that she had not expected to be given a custodial sentence. She didn't even know she was pregnant when she came in, but as part of the new Reception screening process, most of the new residents have a pregnancy test when they arrive, as well as having their urine screened for drugs and alcohol.

I remember how surprised and initially distraught she was when she found out that she was expecting.

She had been charged with conspiracy to supply class A drugs, along with her older and dominant ex-boyfriend. She said that she was aware that he had been involved with dealing drugs in the past, but he had told her he was no longer doing it. She said she was totally unaware that he had drugs hidden in the flat that they shared, until the police raided their property.

'I later found out there were drugs hidden in his sock drawer, and in all his designer trainers in our bedroom – he had loads, rows of 'em,' she told me. 'The first I knew about it was when I was woken up at about six in the morning, with a team of police leaning over me, telling me I was under arrest. I nearly shit myself I was that scared.'

The judge said that it was impossible that she hadn't known that the drugs were there. Megan had sobbed throughout the Reception process, and she was still crying when my Reception shift was over.

I continued to see her from time to time over the next few months, and as her pregnancy advanced, her excitement and hope grew at the rate of her expanding belly, which was wonderful to see. She had been in touch with Birth Companions, a community-based organisation that holds weekly meetings with perinatal women within the prison, who had helped her prepare for motherhood. She was intent on being there for her baby, and being a good mum.

'I feel like one of the lucky ones, being able to have Dylan with me,' Megan said. 'I made an application, and different groups of people decided it was the right decision for me and for him.'

'He knows we're talking about him,' I joked, as Dylan made gentle gurgling and snuffling noises.

We both peered back into the buggy, as he stretched his

arms out from where they had been tucked closely into his chest.

'I want to start afresh. I mean, I'm only 22, and my family have stuck by me and will help me – help both of us – when we get out of here.'

'That's great that your family are so supportive,' I said.

She looked thoughtful.

'It must be so hard for the girls who don't get to look after their babies. There was one girl on the block where I lived, whose baby girl was fostered out because her family wouldn't take her. Her sentence was really long – a few years, I think. She was worried that her daughter might end up being adopted, and she would lose her forever. She was so desperate. It must be heartbreaking.'

When the women are in prison for a long time and there is no family available to help out, babies might go into foster care temporarily until the mother is released, or be adopted with the mother's consent, a process called voluntary adoption.

In some cases, when the sentence is long, the baby will initially be looked after by the mother in the MBU, and then will start to spend increasing amounts of time away from the unit with family members or a foster family, to cause minimal trauma to mother and child. Babies are also taken out of the prison environment regularly, to the local parks and a nearby toddler group, so they can get used to the unfamiliar sights, sounds and smells, and to acclimatise them to life on the outside.

In cases where the baby is taken away from the mother and adopted without their permission – involuntary adoption – the sorrow can understandably be deep and profound and can make it even harder for the women to tackle their addictions and other issues. A powerful stigma exists for women who have been deemed by the courts to be unfit to look after their child or children. It is very hard for everyone involved, but ultimately, the decision always has to be made in the child's best interests. There are many, many people involved in the care of both the mother and the baby. Mothering simply adds a whole new layer of complexity to the female prison experience and there is rarely a perfect solution.

'I see many women in the MBU that have the chance to start afresh,' I told Megan. 'You are doing a great job.'

'I hope so,' she said, smiling and softly stroking Dylan's little hands. 'I just want to move on from my old life. The MBU feels really safe and I'm learning loads. The health visitors are teaching me and the others different things – how to cook, sterilise bottles, and how to get the best out of my playtime with him as he gets older.

'It's great being with the other girls. We're all going through similar stuff, so we understand each other. You should see lunchtimes when we all sit together with the babies. The bigger ones make such as mess – it's absolute carnage!'

I laughed. 'Yes, babies don't often follow the rulebook.' Megan smiled.

Megan had been given a three-year sentence, but would most likely serve eighteen months in custody and the rest on licence – meaning she would spend the remainder of her sentence on the outside, but would need to stick to certain conditions, including keeping in touch with supervising officers, not committing any offences, and residing permanently at one address. This meant that unlike some mothers, hopefully, she wouldn't be split up from her baby. If women come into prison with babies under 18 months old, they can apply for a place on the MBU, and if they get a place, they have all the normal responsibilities of parenting, from changing nappies, to bath-time, playtime and everything in between. Apart from when their babies are in the nursery, the mums are encouraged to be fully responsible for the welfare of their children.

'It never ends,' she told me. 'No telly time for me.'

The mothers are also given the opportunity to shop for their babies' things using a combination of their own funds and child support money. This helps them with issues like budgeting, so that when they return home, buying nappies, formula and other items for their babies would not feel unfamiliar. When Dylan was old enough, Megan would be able to wean him herself, using food she had bought and cooked for him.

'Some of the other mums shop from Asda for their babies. Those Organix toddler biscuits taste so good! They're better than the food they serve us,' Megan chuckled.

The unit also offered a therapeutic environment and

sessions around parenting, as well as practical help. The very regime of prison – the rules, the regularity of food being provided, no drugs, no domestic violence – promotes bonding with children and is ideal for young women like Megan, who need the support.

'The team are so helpful and always have time for us,' she told me. 'I know some of the other residents think we have it easy on the MBU, but we don't. It's a tough graft!'

'It is,' I smiled. 'Being a mum is very hard work!'

I prescribed a course of antibiotics and painkillers on the computer for Megan, so that she could start them straight away, and told her to come back and see me if her symptoms persisted.

'I will,' she said. 'Thank you for seeing me.'

'You're welcome. It was really good to see you again,' I said, and with that she wheeled her buggy and baby out of my little room and off down the corridor.

As I watched her go, a memory flashed into my head of the day I had to go back to work when my first son, Rob, was three months old. Apart from all the usual hormonal and emotional fluctuations of the postnatal rollercoaster ride, I was also struggling to imagine a future for my beloved little boy.

When I was thirty-four weeks pregnant, I was referred for a scan to check the placental flow as my bump was measuring smaller than it should've done at that stage of the pregnancy. I wasn't nervous going to the scan, and I thought it was routine, so I drove there myself. I had seen enough pregnant women to know that the size of the bump often did not reflect the size of the baby. I didn't for a moment imagine there would be anything wrong.

The consultant I was referred to in Oxford was very quiet and seemed to spend an eternity scanning me until he finally announced: 'I can't find his right leg.'

As he said that, my head started spinning and even though I was lying down, I felt as if I was going to pass out.

'What do you mean?' I asked in disbelief, wanting him to say he had made a mistake, that it wasn't true.

He continued in an unemotional way to give me a medical list of other possible problems that Rob may have; complicated syndromes that I had never heard of, that could be associated with a limb not developing.

'But we won't know what else may be wrong with him until he is born,' the consultant said.

As he carried on talking, I became more and more terrified until I convinced myself that my poor little baby was going to face a life of unimaginable difficulties.

I felt as if I couldn't breathe. I don't know how I made it home.

Over the next ten days, my fears spiralled out of control as I imagined all sorts of dreadful scenarios. I couldn't imagine the future and felt like I was living in a nightmare I couldn't wake up from.

I struggled to eat and sleep and even just to think straight in the end.

I lost a stone in weight in that time, and when I felt

that I just couldn't cope any longer the decision was made for me to have a caesarean section when I was thirty-six weeks, as there was a growing concern for both my sanity and Rob's welfare.

I hoped and prayed with all my heart that it would only be his leg that was missing, and that all the fears and dark imaginings that had formed and grown in my mind would not prove to be a reality.

Holding him in my arms and looking into his tiny face for the first time, my love for him was immediately over-whelming, overpowering and beautiful. My fears of multiple problems were unfounded, to my massive relief. But despite my incredible love for him, I thought I could never truly be happy again. He was born with a very short bent right tibia, no fibula, and he only had three little toes on his right foot. It was obvious that he would have to undergo major surgery to enable him to walk, and would forever be dependent on a prosthetic leg.

It is impossible to know, when our children are babies, what the future will hold for them. I shed so many tears in those first few weeks, that I began to wonder if I would ever get through a day without crying. Little did I know then that he would turn out to be one of the happiest and most positive people I have ever met. He loves life with a passion, and after leaving school travelled all over the world with a spare leg in his rucksack. While on his travels he skydived and did the biggest bungee jump in the world with his one leg strapped for safety.

I still remember the dreadful thought of leaving him, and of how nervous I felt about going back to work. I had convinced myself that I had forgotten all the medicine I ever knew, and felt I had lost every tiny grain of confidence I ever possessed, especially as I'd never had much to start with. I felt the same dread of separation and loss of confidence just before going back to work when my beloved second son Charlie was three months old. It was no easier second time around. Even though it was over thirty years ago, the memory was still so clear and vivid.

*

By definition, the fact Bronzefield is a prison for women means it is full of mothers and the human female chains that form our society. Around two-thirds of women in prison have dependent children under the age of 18 at home. There are mothers whose kids have been taken away from them; mothers whose kids are temporarily being looked after by others; new mothers looking after their babies on the MBU; and, sometimes, mothers who have harmed their children.

In many cells are photos of kids – baby photos, school photos, holiday pics – little gummy faces staring down from the confined walls. Alongside these are scrappy bits of paper with drawings of rainbows, cars, princesses, footballs and everything in between; a complete range of children's wonderful creations and imaginings to cheer up their rooms and make them feel a bit more homely.

Around 18,000 children per year are separated from their mothers due to imprisonment, yet only nine per cent of them are cared for by their fathers in their mothers' absence, and only five per cent remain in their own home. One fifth of the mothers in prison were lone parents before imprisonment. The impact must be far-reaching. There is an army of women out there who take on these mothering roles. It may begin with a sudden phone call from the police station or social services. Sometimes it is only when a mother gets to Reception that she will tell an officer that she has left her child or children with a friend or neighbour who will be expecting her to pick them up. What a terrifying thought for a mother to know that she will not be able to see her children, and for her to think of the fear and shock that they may be feeling.

Many women must struggle with their identity as mothers when their children are not with them. How can you be a mother in the truest definition of the word when you are not there to care for them? The separation of mothers and their children is definitely one of the most painful aspects of being in prison for a lot of the women I meet, and the trauma of this severance must cut both ways. There are people whose job it is to aim to improve the ties between mothers and their children, but once mothers are in prison, it must be really difficult.

*

I was driving into prison to work a Saturday afternoon shift, and I could see a wide variety of people of all ages and ethnicities arriving to visit friends and loved ones. Some people were being pushed in wheelchairs, some had walking aids and appeared to struggle to walk, but they were all there to support the person they cared about.

As I drove up to the prison, I reflected that many of these people may have travelled a long way, and by that time the children and elderly guests might be exhausted and running on pure nerves. I could see babies being pushed in buggies along the pavements and young children skipping and laughing with excitement at the thought of seeing the person they loved. It was a strangely heart-warming sight, but at the same time it was also quite sad and thought-provoking. It was hard to imagine the huge range of emotions everyone might feel in that single day: from excitement, heightened anticipation and apprehension before the visit, to joy and happiness at being reunited, through to profound sadness and grief at being parted again. I imagined there would be many tears shed later in the day when it came to saying goodbye.

As I was pulling into a parking space, I noticed an elderly lady who appeared to be struggling a bit to get out of her car a few spaces along from me. I could see that she was on her own and so I offered her a helping hand, which she graciously accepted.

She asked if I could pass her walking stick and handbag out of the car.

'It's my arthritis,' she said. 'I can walk, I just find long distances hard and it can be quite a trek across this car park.'

'Yes, I know it can, and it's worse on a miserable old rainy day like this,' I said. 'Are you here for a visit?'

'Yes, to see my daughter, Denise. She's been here for four years. Are you here for a visit too?'

'No, I work here. I'm due to start at two,' I explained.

The lady told me that she had spent the last four years as the sole carer for her twin nine-year-old grandsons, after her daughter and her daughter's partner were both imprisoned. She didn't tell me what their crime was, and I didn't like to ask.

'We'd been led to believe that they wouldn't be given a custodial sentence, so it came as a massive shock,' she explained. 'It just doesn't seem right to take a mum from her kids, but I s'pose that's what happens if you get on the wrong side of the law.'

Sometimes women arrive in prison while their children are still at school, not for a minute even thinking they would be given a custodial sentence when they set off for court that day. They would more likely be thinking about what they would be serving their kids for tea. Similarly, there would be children up and down the country at school expecting to go home as normal, without any idea that it would be someone different picking them up. There are no tearful goodbyes, just separation, cutting through their lives as sharp as a knife.

'I never thought I'd end up looking after young kids at my age though,' the woman continued. 'It's so exhausting but I love 'em to bits. Every day of her trial, I sat listening and waiting, hoping with all my heart for a good outcome. It wasn't to be.

'On the day she was sentenced and led away, the only two thoughts I had were, "How am I going to tell the children?" and "How on earth am I going to cope?" I was devastated.

'But I couldn't just turn my back on them and say I wasn't going to look after them.

'The boys were only five at the time. When their mum was sent away, I picked them up from school and they came back with me. We felt invisible. I went from being their nan to their parents but there was no way they were going to go into care. They are my grandsons; I was determined that was not going to happen. Heaven forbid.'

We started walking slowly towards the entrance where the Visitors' Centre is located next to the staff entrance.

'How are they doing? Are you coping okay?' I asked.

'They're alright on the whole I suppose, but they have definitely been affected. I know, deep down, they're hurting. I try to reassure them as much as I can. At first, I wasn't sure how much to tell them, and just told them that their mum still loves them but she had to go away for making a mistake. They're a bit older now, so I try to be honest with them about what's happening and why. But I'm never sure whether it's too much or too little. I mean, I'm no professional.'

Many women have told me that they simply do not tell their kids they are in prison. They weave elaborate stories about being in hospital, working away from home, or joining the Army. One 63-year-old resident told me that she had told her five-year-old granddaughter that she was in Wales painting a castle for the next six months.

'It's just easier that way,' they say to me. 'No need for them to deal with the reality. It's all very well us being here, but they have to deal with it out there. Go to school and hear people gossip. I don't want to put them through that.'

'You can only do your best,' I told the lady as we walked through the car park, hoping to reassure her a little.

'Trouble is, other people get to know your situation and the boys have been badly bullied by some of the kids at school, and on the street where we live,' she explained. 'Kieron still wets the bed. I've been into school loads of times to try and sort it out, and they say they will, but it still happens. They still get bullied.

'They're on a trip today with the Cubs, but I try to bring them to see her as much as I can, to keep the relationship going, but it can be hard as the visits are a bit difficult sometimes. Occasionally Kieron doesn't want to come with us. He's quite angry about everything. Again, between school and me, we're doing our best to help him, but he lashes out at us and I know his behaviour is bad. As he grows up it's getting worse. I worry that they're going to end up going down the same road as their mum. That would totally destroy me. I think the world of them.

'She calls us as much as possible, but it can be a struggle to know what to talk about sometimes. She's got a job, and has done some education courses, and she seems to be doing her best to make a better life, so she can support the boys when she comes out. I hope so, but it might take me a lot of time to trust her again.

'I try to give them a normal life as best I can but it's hard,' she said. 'Money's tight, too. I had some savings, but it's all gone so it's really tough now. We've had to use food banks before.'

'Do you manage to come and visit much?' I asked her.

'I've only been once this month. We live over two hours away, and the petrol's so expensive. Sometimes I just can't afford it,' she said.

'Oh, that must be really hard for you,' I said, trying to imagine how on earth she managed to cope.

'But on the whole the kids enjoy visiting and love playing with all the stuff they have here. It feels pretty informal and I always give them two pounds each for snacks. They have to go through quite a lot of security, of course, but they always get a big hug off their mum, and I think that's probably the best bit for them,' she added.

'It must be wonderful for them to have a lovely hug from Mum, and even better for her. I bet she looks forward to that more than anything else,' I replied, knowing how comforting a loving hug can be.

As we arrived at the entrance to the prison, we wished each other a happy day and went our separate ways, but I found myself thinking about how challenging life must be for those two boys and their grandmother.

*

The number of visits each resident is allowed from family members and friends is determined via their status, which is based on behaviour. There is an Incentives policy in place, so if prisoners work hard, stick to the rules and exceed behaviour expectations, they can improve their status. There are three levels: Bronze, Silver and Gold. New residents go to prison on Silver and it can take them as little as eight weeks to achieve Gold status. Commendations are given out for good behaviour and with three commendations they can receive Gold, which leads to additional privileges, such as an increase in the amount of money that can be sent in, access to Avon beauty catalogues and quarterly social events. If residents get two behavioural warnings, they have a meeting with a senior officer to discuss what is going on and to see if they need additional support or help. After that meeting, if they get one further warning, there is an official review, which could lead to demotion. There is now an add-on scheme called Incentives Plus. If a resident gets five commendations in a month, they are eligible for an additional privilege, which could be access to the Vita Nova café, a free eyebrow shape at Shades of Beauty, an additional £5 from their private cash allowance, or a visit in the private family room. This system recently replaced the older IEP (Incentives and Earned Privileges) scheme, where the levels were known as Basic, Standard and Enhanced, but the premise is the same, and many still refer to the previous terminology. At Bronzefield, Silver residents can book a maximum of four visits per month, and Gold residents can book a maximum of six visits per month, all of which can be of two hours in duration.

Some manage to get visits regularly, but sometimes it may be much less frequent, possibly months before they can see their children due to the distance the family have to travel and the expense that involves. Certainly, for most women, these visits are what they live for and gives them hope and purpose – a shining light of joy on the horizon.

There are fewer women's prisons in the country as a whole, so the average distance for a female inmate from her home to Bronzefield is around fifty-five miles. But they are at the mercy of the system, and an eight-hour round trip for a family to see their loved one is not unusual. Having a mother in prison can stretch what may already be fairly tight finances even thinner. Families may lose the income generated by a woman if she had been working, and extended family members such as grandparents may be forced to give up work or cut down their hours to care for children. Other factors that might stop visits include the fact that they may be scheduled for when children should be at school, or they have no adult to accompany them because their guardians are working.

There are family support workers on hand to help

promote familial relationships, and to ease the stress of what must be quite an unusual setting for mothers to see their children. In real life, it's not often that we sit opposite loved ones and talk constantly, but the reality of these visits is that prisoners and families sit across a table and probably try to maintain conversation about 'normal' things – especially if children are present – and that they may feel awkward if they can't keep the conversation going. Residents can apply for a visit in the family room, so they are not surrounded by other visits, but the same rules apply.

The prison also runs family days every other month in the gym, open to all residents regardless of their privilege level. These visits coincide with school holidays and have themes, depending on the time of year, with a big party around Christmas, filled with presents, excitement and talk of Santa's visit.

These days are undoubtedly a huge highlight for many mothers behind bars, but they must also be a very bittersweet reminder of what they are missing.

Chapter Three

'She's still my little girl...'

Most mothers will do anything for their children and this must be one of the strongest bonds that humans share. A bond that lasts a lifetime.

One day two women arrived together to be seen in my clinic. It wasn't unusual for someone coming to see me to bring a friend with them. Some residents are paid to help care for others, and some act as advocates, to help patients get their point across or to help them understand the details of their care.

Both women were bottle blonde with delicately upturned noses and heart-shaped faces. Sophie had a slight frame and long limbs – she looked like she could sprint fast if she needed to. Helen was slightly rounder and had clear worry lines between her brows and fine crow's feet around her eyes, but it was clear from the moment I set eyes on them that they were related.

'I hope you don't mind me bringing Soph too,' Helen said. 'She's my daughter and she's been worrying about me. She really wanted me to come in and see you today. I've been getting these awful headaches, mainly at the back of my head, but the pain goes right over the top...' She gestured up towards her head. 'They usually get worse through the day and paracetamol doesn't help much.'

'And she had this weird turn the other evening,' Sophie added. 'We share a cell and it was around 9 p.m. We'd been locked up for the night. I was trying to tell her something and she went all stiff and strange, like she wasn't all there. I thought she was having some sort of fit. She had something similar a while back, but I thought she was messing about, so when it happened again it really frightened me.'

I asked Helen more questions about her headaches. She said there was no change in her vision, that she had never vomited with them, and that they were never there when she woke up. There was no history of migraines in the family that she knew of.

'Do you remember what happened that evening?' I asked her.

'Not really,' Helen replied. 'I remember feeling a bit headachey and not quite myself. It's hard to describe really. '

'And how are you feeling generally?'

'Okay, mostly.'

I put the cuff around her arm to take her blood pressure – it was fine, and she looked well.

'It's difficult to know exactly what has caused these strange turns that you've had, so the safest way forward would be to refer you to a neurologist who can do the necessary investigations,' I told her.

'What could it be?' Helen asked nervously.

'The chances are it won't be anything serious,' I reassured her. 'But we have to rule out the remote possibility of a small space-occupying lesion. Or as most people would call it, a brain tumour.'

'Really?' Sophie chipped in, looking horrified, her hand over her mouth, white skin stretched over her knuckles.

'I promise you that the chances of it being anything bad are really, really low,' I told her. 'Please try not to worry. In all my years of medicine, of all the people I have referred for similar symptoms, I think I can only remember about four people who actually had a brain tumour. But I wouldn't be doing my job properly if I didn't refer you.'

My words seemed to calm them down.

We all sat in silence for a second or two.

'It must be wonderful to have each other for support,' I said.

'Yes, it's great, even though she drives me mad sometimes trying to "look after" me. But I'm glad we're together in here,' Sophie said. 'It makes it so much easier.'

Helen cackled: 'Me look after you? What's today all about then?'

The women laughed easily together. As Sophie leaned towards her mother, I glimpsed a small yellow and black bumblebee on her wrist.

'I like your tattoo,' I commented.

'It stands for personal power and loyalty,' she said, 'And demanding work – I've always worked really hard and had jobs. Ever since I was 14. Mum's got one too... show the doctor, Mum.'

Helen peeled back the sleeve of her jumper, to reveal a matching inking.

'Sophie really wanted me to have one too,' she said. 'At first, I wasn't sure. I don't really like tattoos much, and thought I was a bit old to have one, but I'm glad I did.' She pulled a face. 'Hurt like hell, though,' she said.

'Time's passing a bit quicker 'cos we have each other, isn't it, Mum?' Sophie added.

Helen nodded.

'I'm busy getting my Level 2 qualification at the gym, and Mum's in the laundry, but there is still a lot of time when we're not at work,' Sophie continued.

'We just try to keep ourselves to ourselves,' Helen added.

I wondered why they were both in prison together. 'Did you spend much time in the gym before prison?' I asked.

'Not really, but I always had to be fit for work.'

'What did you do?'

'I was a paramedic. We live together, just Mum and me. She was a teaching assistant at the local school. It's just the two of us at home. Dad died when I was small and Al, my brother, he lives in London. We've always enjoyed spending time together, haven't we, Mum?'

'She's great company,' Helen replied. 'We often go shopping or for a few drinks. I know it's a cliché, but Soph really is my best friend.'

'I'd been qualified as a paramedic for three years,' Sophie continued. 'Mum kept telling me to take up teaching but I'm no good with kids. That's her job. I liked the idea of studying medicine but didn't fancy spending five years at university. I didn't get the grades for medicine either, so I thought being a paramedic would be the perfect job for me and it was. It was really exciting and rewarding, and I loved it. I always wanted to do some sort of medical job so I could help other people.'

I understood how she felt.

I knew from around the age of seven that I wanted to be a doctor. After that, I could never imagine any other life, and was grateful when I was growing up that I knew what I wanted to do, unlike most of my friends who hadn't got a clue. I had something to hope and work for.

My father was a GP and I thought he had the perfect job. He set up his own practice in Wexham Road in Slough, an area where there was a lot of poverty at the time. He bought a little semi-detached house and we lived upstairs, and he had his surgery downstairs, where he and his patients would often consult while smoking one of his 'Players' cigarettes that he would offer them.

It was the 1950s, and there wasn't much money around then because it wasn't long after the war. In those days, a chicken was a real treat to have for dinner. In the run-up to Christmas, he would make up food hampers with a fresh chicken and lots of other treats, and he would give them to some of his elderly and lonely patients who had nothing. It was his Christmas present to them, and possibly the only one they would receive.

On Christmas Eve I would travel with him in his little Morris Minor 1000 car to deliver the parcels. I can vividly remember standing in their tiny little pre-fabricated houses, and seeing the joy he brought to those people and how his kindness and generosity made such a difference to them. I was just a child, but I knew that was how I wanted to live my life. I knew that if I was lucky enough to be able to help people who were less fortunate, I would. It left a lasting impression on me.

I adored my parents and was fascinated by my father's job. Whenever I was allowed to at weekends, I used to go out on his visits with him. I would sit in the car and wait for him, and as soon as he climbed back in, I would quiz him about the people he had seen. He would talk to me about medicine and the people he saw, and even though I was very unlikely to meet them or know them, I was captivated by the day-to-day stories of their lives.

I was also fascinated by his medical case. It had little drawers in it containing bottles of pills, glass ampoules, syringes and needles. There were also prescription pads, pens and writing paper, and it had a sharp and distinctive but hard-to-describe smell; a mixture of old leather and chemicals.

As soon as I qualified, I was determined to get myself a bag just like it.

'I know just what you mean, Sophie,' I said. 'It's a calling, isn't it?'

She nodded. 'I spent three years training to be a para-medic. They called me the "Heart Attack Queen". If there was a cardiac arrest, I'm your girl.' She waved across my desk and grinned. 'These hands might be small, but I do mean chest compressions.'

I smiled.

'I found it really rewarding but I'm not going to lie – it was pretty tough at times.'

'The hours were really long,' Helen added. 'She was always tired and stressed. It was hard to see her like that. She lost loads of weight and often used to come home completely knackered.'

Sophie nodded. 'I've had my hair pulled and been kicked and punched by aggressive patients. I know some of them are so out of it they don't know what they're doing. But I'm only little, and so they always partnered me with one of the heavier guys. My favourite is called Jim – he's what I like to call a "unit". There was nothing going to get past him.'

I felt for her. I think to do a job like that you would have to be pretty tough and brave. Before my time at Bronzefield, I worked at Wormwood Scrubs for seven years, so I knew how she felt to be a woman faced with a man twice your size, even though, strangely, I rarely felt scared.

'I was getting used to seeing it all,' she said. 'Shaving cuts, toothaches, people locked in the toilet, you name it, we would've handled it. The drunks, the idiots, the timewasters. Many people just saw us as a taxi to hospital, I think.'

Helen rolled her eyes. 'It's hard to think that someone might die 'cos someone else is attention-seeking.'

Sophie continued: 'There was this one guy on our patch, near where we live. He rung constantly, and I ended up taking him to hospital maybe five times. He's a youngish guy but is pretty overweight, and was always complaining that he had chest pain. There was never anything seriously wrong, as far as I could tell. I felt a bit sorry for him really. It was tough, especially when we could hear on the radios that we were needed somewhere else. Frustrating doesn't really cover it.'

I could sympathise with Sophie. When I was a GP in the community, a lot of my friends who worked for the ambulance service told me of their frustration with people who would ring up to twenty times a day. I have even known of people being sent to prison for abuse of the emergency services with unnecessary calls.

'I was often stressed,' Sophie continued. 'I think most jobs come with a fair amount of pressure, but it took me a while to get into it and not let every person I'd treated affect me. Sometimes the stories stick with you. I found it hard to switch off.'

I knew exactly what that felt like, too. At times, it can be so hard to stop thinking of some of the sad stories and tragedies encountered in a day-to-day job working in the service sector.

'We were out one Friday night, having a few drinks in the pub, trying to unwind after a busy week. Just minding our own business. When I saw him, I couldn't believe it. What are the chances? He just sauntered in with a mate of his, like they owned the place. As soon as I saw him, Mum and I drank up – we were ready to leave anyway as we'd had a fair bit by then. It was time to call it a night. I knew he recognised me. He was shouting, "Oi, blondie!" He followed us down the road and kept heckling.

'He'd called me that a few times when we'd been out to see him. I always ignored him. Once, in the ambulance, he grabbed my leg and I had to bat his hand away. I didn't say anything. I knew if I told Jim, he would hit the roof, and tell me that I needed to report it.

'That night, it felt different. It was out of the context of work and there was no Jim around for back-up. He was looking for trouble. He went for me, and Mum went for him. That's when it all went wrong.'

Helen folded her arms, her expression firm and defiant. 'It was a scuffle that went wrong, you could say. He started on Soph and I hit back. I just saw red and tore into him. Simple as that; I know she's grown up but she's still my little girl and she was half the size of that fat bastard... I'm still not sorry—'

'Mum, don't... .' Sophie cut in.

'But I'm not. He deserved what he got. We were done for ABH.'

'We got two years each,' Sophie added. 'I hope we'll be out on tag soon. We've both served nine months. I won't be able to go back to the ambulance service, so I've been doing my gym qualifications – I want to work as an instructor when I get out. There's a big gym near where we live.'

'That sounds much less stressful Sophie,' I said, momentarily imagining what a nice job that would be.

I'd seen the gym at the prison, and knew it was a good place for Sophie to get started. It is kitted out with all sorts of equipment: cycling machines, rowing and running machines and weights. As well as classes, the girls and women are encouraged by civilian instructors to do a qualification across a number of weeks, so they can teach after their release from prison.

'It's great,' Sophie smiled. 'I've been supporting a lot of other residents with their physio exercises and the like. I still feel like I'm making a difference and doing something meaningful. It's just different.'

Helen looked over at Sophie and smiled proudly. But then she frowned and screwed up her nose. 'I'm not sure what I'm going to do. Obviously, I won't be able to go back into the school. That's going to be hard. No doubt all the neighbours will know about us. I imagine we've been the talk of the town, but I hope they'll be alright with us when we get home.'

I was fascinated by their story and saddened by it too. I felt it was such a shame that two seemingly lovely people had lost their careers due to a random crazy situation that had spiralled out of control.

'I will write a referral letter to the hospital,' I told her. 'Your appointment will come through. You won't know the date, but the officers will come and take you there. Please can you come and see me after you've been to the hospital to let me know how you get on? I'm sure it's going to be fine.'

'Great, thank you so much for your time today and for taking me seriously,' Helen replied.

'It was really good to meet you both,' I said. 'I hope everything goes well.'

'Thanks,' they replied in sync, similar relieved expressions on their faces.

*

Sometimes, of course, women are in prison for a horrific reason and occasionally I come across a case that truly shocks me to the core.

One Tuesday morning, as I was scanning the appointment ledger for the day ahead, Kate, one of the nurses, popped her head around the door.

'Morning, Doctor Brown,' she said, her face unusually glum. Kate was normally always ready with a funny quip for most situations, but her expression was cold and hard.

'Morning, Kate. Are you okay?'

'Not great,' she said. 'There's someone in Healthcare who we have to see this morning. Her name is Hannah.' Kate paused. 'She's been accused of murdering her child.'

I felt sick when she told me, and a sharp pain shot through my chest. I thought of my precious sons and of the overwhelming love I have for them.

'Apparently, she told the officers that she was trying to spare her son a life of hell.'

For a couple of minutes, we were both silent, lost in our own painful thoughts.

When there is a case like this, of a child being hurt, it affects everyone involved in that resident's care, including the nurses, officers and other members of staff.

I have known a number of people who think that working in a prison will be exciting and challenging, but unfortunately find out quite quickly that the reality of the brutality and rawness of the place is simply too much for them, and they decide to move on to a different career, often within a matter of months, or even weeks.

However, some staff like Kate had been doing the job for years, and despite the difficult and varied challenges she had faced during her time, she loved her job and the community within the prison. It definitely takes a certain type of person to cope with working in a prison and she was one of them. Before working in Bronzefield, she had worked as a midwife for many years in a nearby hospital, but when her children had grown up and left home, she decided that she wanted a new challenge and saw a job advertised at Bronzefield and decided to give it go. That was ten years ago and from that day on she still, somehow, found the strength to carry on.

I decided to go and see Hannah before the clinic was due to start at 10 a.m. Due to the nature of her crime, she had been placed on constant watch on the Healthcare wing.

There was concern that once the reality of what she had done kicked in, she could be at serious risk of self-harm. A seventeen-bed facility, the Healthcare wing has twenty-four-hour supervision for residents that are too unwell, either mentally or physically, to be on normal location. An ACCT (Assessment Care in Custody and Teamwork) book is opened on anyone thought to be at risk of self-harm. This is a care planning process and requires that certain actions are taken within different timeframes to ensure that the risk of self-harm and suicide is reduced. The frequency of the checks depends on the level of risk, and can range from checks two or three times a day to constant watch, which entails a member of staff sitting outside their cell and observing the resident continuously twenty-four hours a day. I still remember my surprise many years ago when I first saw someone sitting outside a gated prisoner's cell in Wormwood Scrubs at 10 o'clock at night when I was going home. I asked him what time his shift was finishing, and he told me he would be there until his replacement took over at 8 a.m. the following day.

I have walked along the Healthcare corridor countless times, never knowing what I would be met with. It can get extremely noisy at times if a resident decides to protest by banging on their door all day long, with anything they can find to make enough noise. A shoe, their plastic cup, or anything else they may have to hand.

Sometimes they may just scream for hours on end, which can make it feel as if I am in a horror film.

At other times they may go on dirty protests and smear faeces around the walls, window and floor of their cell. Some of them occasionally use dirty sanitary towels to cover up the hatch in the cell door, to stop the officers or nurses looking in to check on them. One resident decided to put her CPAP machine – a medical device to help with breathing at night – in the loo and defaecate on it. It can be an extremely difficult and challenging place in which to work and also to be located.

I locked my door behind me, and Kate and I set off to see Hannah in Healthcare. That day it felt unusually quiet and sombre. We could even hear our shoes clicking on the lino floor.

We went in to see the officers first to ask permission to see her, and then we all walked along to her room. My stomach was churning as they tapped on the door to announce our arrival, before unlocking the big heavy metal door. As I entered the room Hannah was sitting at the small desk writing in a notebook with her head bowed. The winter sun was shining brightly through the little window on the cold January morning, casting a shard of light across her head. The television was on with the volume turned right down, just providing a picture in the background.

'Hello, Hannah, I'm Doctor Brown. I'm just here to see if you're okay and whether you need any medication prescribing. Were you taking any regular medication before you came to prison?' I asked her. I concentrated desperately on trying not to think about what she had done.

She just looked like any other resident. She was in her late twenties and wearing a tracksuit and trainers. Her jet black hair was a bit messy. She looked up and we locked eyes. There were certainly no histrionics or even tears. She was calm, polite and quietly spoken, but was clearly not keen to engage in conversation.

'Yeah, I'm fine, I don't need any medication, thanks,' she replied and turned back to her writing.

What do you say? I wondered if she was completely in shock. Had the reality of what she had done sunk in yet? Would it ever?

I still felt sick. I couldn't help but imagine the horror of what she must have been going through. How her poor little boy would have suffered in those moments.

As I turned to leave, I began to question whether I could carry on much longer with this job, unsure how much more sadness I could cope with. Maybe it was finally time to walk away and admit defeat.

I know that my job is not to judge and that when I took the Hippocratic Oath I vowed to care for 'all my fellow human beings, those sound of mind and body, as well as the infirm,' but this was one of the very rare times that I found myself really battling to do so.

As I left her room, I passed the chaplain waiting to go in. *His job must be even more difficult than mine*, I thought. I couldn't imagine how challenging it must be to offer pastoral care to all those in need. How could he possibly comfort and support someone who had done something so awful?

But he was his usual calm, gentle and serene self as he went in to do his best to bring some comfort to her.

Kate and I walked back in total silence. I had to try to put all thoughts of tragedy firmly behind me. It was time to start my clinic, but I just couldn't shake off the overwhelming sadness I was feeling.

Chapter Four

'You! Miss Brown, to the board'

Whenever I can, I try to show the women at Bronzefield that I do believe that they can rebuild their lives. I try to be a kind, listening ear when everything may seem pretty bleak. For the most part they know that, whenever possible, I am on their side. In all walks of life there are bullies and tyrants, and it is easy to be damaged by words and actions from others, but there are those who may support you and all it takes is an unexpected ally to flip a story on its head. When you are backed into a corner and someone champions and believes in you, it can change your life.

I was born in the London Hospital in Whitechapel (now the Royal London Hospital) and I am very proud of my East End roots. By all accounts, my great-grandfather was quite a character and had a pub in Limehouse, where sailors from all around the world would trade a small treasure from their home country for food, beer, and shelter if needed, and Charlie Brown's pub became a very popular haven for many a lost soul. He was a kind and honest man, from reports I have read, and even became a governor of the hospital.

My mother had suffered from so many miscarriages that when at last my sister was born, she didn't think that she would be able to have any more children, especially as she was nearing forty years of age by then, and back in those days it was regarded as dangerous to have children 'late in life'. But along I popped nearly three years after my sister, in 1954. Growing up in the fifties and sixties, career choices for women were very limited, with the expectation that my friends and I would be nurses, secretaries or teachers. I grew up always knowing that I wanted to be a doctor. I had to work extremely hard, and never really believed in myself, but I just wanted it so, so badly I couldn't imagine any other way to live my life.

My father worked so hard as a doctor that it took a toll on his health, but he loved his job and cared deeply for his patients. His compassion for others and his passion for medicine shaped my life.

When I said that I wanted to be a doctor I was advised by my teachers that it would be too difficult and that it was a career much more suited to men. But I was determined not to be talked out of pursuing my dream and so knuckled down. I became a bit of a recluse. The only place I could hide away with my books at home was in an eaves cupboard, which was just big enough to fit a small desk, lamp and chair, and it became my little haven. But the dark clouds of self-doubt were never far away.

I was dreading my A levels as my whole future depended on getting good enough grades. When they were over, I spent the summer holiday working as a cleaner in the local hospital, but by the time the results came out, I had convinced myself that I had failed the lot. When I found out that I had achieved the results I needed to go to medical school, it felt like I had won the lottery. Many of my friends were leaving school and getting married and having children, but I knew that I wanted to be a doctor more than anything else.

I started training at the London Hospital in 1973. I thought I would be in a white coat and on the wards from day one, but the first two years were spent studying Anatomy, Physiology and Biochemistry, in preparation for second MB exams. The exams at the end of the second year were a bit of a watershed because if anyone failed, they were only given one chance to retake them, and if they failed a second time, they were asked to leave. However far I got on my journey towards being a doctor, I always felt I was a hair's breadth away from failure, but to my overwhelming joy and relief I passed and was allowed to continue on my journey.

It was during my finals that I came across someone who wanted to knock me down. Professor Anderson was in his late fifties and one of the senior surgeons at the hospital at the time.

He was incredibly strict, and inspired fear and awe in students in equal measure. A small man with sharp features and piercing blue eyes, he stood so straight that I thought he must have a metal rod down his jacket. He wore starched white shirts with a detachable rigid collar, and the white coat he wore was always pristine; he was so steely and severe that his very presence was intimidating. He was also 'old school' and made it clear that he did not approve of women studying medicine. In my year, twenty-five per cent of us were female; this was twenty-five per cent too many for the Prof. He was one of life's bullies.

During my final year, I was allocated to Prof Anderson's surgical 'firm' to try to revise and learn as much surgery as possible in the run-up to the exams. One senior student was appointed to each firm along with eight junior students.

In one of his terrifying tutorials, I was summoned by him from my seat at the back of the room.

He fixed his icy stare and pointed at me and said: 'You! Miss Brown, to the board. Write out eight causes of a lump in the groin.'

My heart started to race as I walked to the blackboard on the wall behind his desk, aware of the nine pairs of eyes watching me.

He swivelled round in his chair to watch my shaky hand write out one cause after another, so relieved that I knew the answers. I thought I had satisfied him and done okay, but when I had finished writing out the list, he proceeded to interrogate me, asking more and more difficult questions until I ran out of answers.

'Tell me more about a psoas abscess,' he demanded. I had no more answers to give him.

He had pushed me into a corner and all I could do was stare at my feet, my face burning with shame.

He swivelled back to face the junior students and continued to address them, but left me standing at the front of the room and completely ignored me for the rest of the tutorial.

It felt like an eternity. He may as well have plonked a dunce's cap on my head just to add to my shame.

I was left voiceless and humiliated. My self-doubt resurged with a vengeance and I just couldn't imagine overcoming the last hurdle and getting through the final exams. For days and weeks after, his harsh face and my shame filled my daytime thoughts and even my dreams, to the point that I thought I would never be free of him.

I began to have panic attacks.

Every day when I got off the tube at Whitechapel and crossed the road to the hospital, I would feel the symptoms descend like a mist and overtake me. My heart would start to race, my hands would become clammy and my mouth would get so dry it was almost sore. My breathing would be so fast that I became light-headed and dizzy and it felt at times as if I was going to pass out.

Somehow though, I continued to study, but my future felt so uncertain and fragile. I just didn't know how I would ever complete my training and get through finals. Some days, it felt impossible, and I felt so lonely and dejected.

To my horror, about four weeks later, I was summoned to see the Dean of the medical school. He was responsible for all the students and was an almost God-like presence, but he had very little day-to-day involvement with any student, unless they were utterly brilliant – or in big trouble.

I certainly knew that I was not in the brilliant category, and so my fear of what was to come was overwhelming. My catastrophising kicked in and took over. I was going to be asked to leave. I was convinced of it.

All my worst fears were coming true.

As I entered the Dean's large, imposing office, with its dark wooden panels and portraits of important-looking people with lofty expressions all around the room, he was sitting facing me in a large leather chair behind an enormous mahogany desk. I felt numb with fear.

I had never even seen him before, but he had a very kind, round face and smiled gently at me as he asked me to sit down.

'Thank you for coming to see me, Miss Brown,' he said. 'I have had to ask you to come along today as Professor Anderson has said that he does not think you are fit to sit your final exams.'

My heart felt as if it had stopped beating, and a sharp pain shot through my chest.

My world was crumbling. My hopes and dreams fluttering away with those few simple words.

'But,' he continued, 'I know that you are going to pass. What's more I believe that you will make a great success of your career in medicine... And I would like you to work for my firm as my Houseman after qualifying.'

I thought I was dreaming. Not only did he believe in me,

but he was offering me a job as well. I felt ecstatic and so grateful for the opportunity he was giving me.

I stammered a reply. 'I can't think of anything I'd love more. Thank you, sir.'

As I left his room and shut the big heavy door behind me, I felt like I was floating on a cloud.

Forty years on, I have never forgotten the belief that wonderful man had in me, and how a bully had nearly destroyed me. I really do think that is one of the reasons I have always, ever since, tried to champion people that others have tried to destroy, or who have never had anyone that truly believed in them. I hate bullies with a passion and feel lucky now to be in a position that enables me to stand up for people that may have been downtrodden, and possibly misjudged.

Ever since that day, I have been overtly aware of the importance of the words we use and the startling difference kindness can make to anyone, especially when people are at their most vulnerable. By the time they are in prison, many are likely to feel lost, lonely and frightened, and may think they have been treated unfairly. I am surprised how often even the smallest kindness can carry a disproportionate weight.

*

After finishing all my training, I worked as a GP for twenty years in the community, meeting people from all ages and stages of life and from widely differing backgrounds. I really loved my job and felt privileged to be involved with the lives of so many interesting people. It gave me a purpose, and I had worked very hard to build up my practice. It was with a very heavy heart that I resigned in 2004, when a new GP contract meant a way of working I just couldn't believe in – more about targets than the patients. My move to work in prisons almost happened by accident, when I was approached by someone recruiting doctors to work in prisons, and I was overjoyed and excited at the thought of a new challenge.

I spent the first five years after leaving my practice working at Huntercombe young offenders institution, followed by seven years at Wormwood Scrubs. During those years, I was repeatedly advised to avoid working in a female prison. I was told that I was likely to find it much more challenging, due in part to the reputedly very high incidence of self-harm and the emotional fragility of the women, resulting largely from the abuse so many of them had endured. I was also led to believe that the women might resent me and would give me a tough time.

'Men are more straightforward and easier to deal with,' I was told over and over again.

I loved my time in the Scrubs, but there was a dark and debilitating problem spreading through the prison like an epidemic: spice. This psychoactive substance was rife in the prison, and made most of the men who used it unpredictable and dangerous. I didn't know how to help them. There was no treatment I could offer to reverse the dreadful effects it sometimes had. Some just got high, some became overly sedated, and others had terrible seizures. Some men became acutely psychotic, which could make their behaviour wild and very frightening. There was no telling how they may react, which as far as I was concerned made it too dangerous to continue working there as a duty doctor. Sadly, I decided that my time there was over.

As another chapter in my life came to an end, I decided to face what I thought might be my final demon, and agreed to try working in a female prison. From all the stories and warnings I'd heard, I thought that I would probably only manage the few sessions I had agreed to work before moving on elsewhere. But to my relief, my preconceptions and misgivings proved to be totally unfounded. I loved it. At first, I struggled to believe that many of the women I was meeting had committed a crime at all, as by far the majority of them were so friendly and welcoming.

Bronzefield is the largest female prison in Europe, and the only purpose-built prison solely for women. It is one of only two prisons in the UK to house Category A prisoners, otherwise known as 'restricted' status. This means it houses those people deemed to pose the most threat to the public, police or national security, should they escape.

It opened in 2004, and has housed some of the UK's most dangerous prisoners, including extremist Roshonara Choudhry, who stabbed MP Stephen Timms, in 2010, and others like Mairead Philpott who, along with her husband Mick and friend Paul Mosley, was found guilty of starting a fire that killed six of her children in 2012.

Previous residents also include Karen Matthews, who faked the kidnapping of her daughter Shannon, and Tracey Connelly, who was sent to prison after admitting causing or allowing the death of her son, Peter, known during the case as Baby P.

Life imprisonment is a sentence that lasts until the death of the prisoner, but they will normally be eligible for parole (officially termed 'early release') after a fixed period set by the judge. This is called minimum term – however, in the most serious and barbaric crimes, judges may order a life sentence that means life, known as a 'whole life order'. The only two women in the UK who have been served with a whole life order, Rosemary West and serial killer Joanna Dennehy, have both spent time at Bronzefield.

The operational capacity of HMP Bronzefield is 572, with the residents housed across four different wings referred to as house blocks, as well as the Mother and Baby unit, and Phoenix House (a ten-bedded unit offering semi-open conditions). There are around 130 prisoners in each house block. It is a complete contrast to the Scrubs, which is a vast Victorian prison holding about 1300 men in a building that is dramatic, imposing, and possibly intimidating to anyone not familiar with the place. When I first saw the building and grounds, Bronzefield felt so bright and modern in comparison, almost like an ugly leisure centre from the outside – if you didn't look up and see the barbed wire curled along the fencing and the colossal gates that allowed the prison vans in and out. There is even a garden in the centre of the house blocks, and the first time I saw it I was struck by how well tended it was.

House Block One is the detox wing, which houses women who have a history of alcohol and drug addiction. When they first arrive in prison, they may be very unwell due to withdrawal from alcohol and/or whatever drugs they may have been using, and so there are more nurses on site to assist with medication and issues associated with withdrawal.

House Block Two is the induction wing, where women who do not have a history of substance misuse are located when they first arrive in custody. For women who have never been in prison before this is particularly important, as the officers go through the different aspects of prison life, and explain things such as how to use the electronic kiosk systems called pods, through which they order their food, seek healthcare appointments and order their canteen, which includes the treats they can buy with money earned. They are also shown how to get a pin number for the phone, apply for jobs, or to attend the gym, as well as how to apply for healthcare appointments. This may be with the GP, dentist, podiatrist, well-women clinic, sexual health clinic, mental health team, substance misuse clinic, nurse triage, or pharmacy clinic, if they want to discuss their medication.

On induction, residents are assessed in English and maths using computers, and all women who score below a certain level are required to engage in education, before they can apply for a job.

House Block Three predominantly accommodates sentenced prisoners, whilst House Block Four is for prisoners serving life and long-term sentences, as well as those on an enhanced regime.

On this block, there are no bars or gates between the spurs, there are some cells with showers and there is a small, separate garden.

Each house block looks identical with a central office and four spurs – A, B, C and D – fanning off the central corridor, with cells located along each side. There are two floors on each block. Meals are served on each spur, and residents socialise in the central areas.

Most prisoners live in single cells, but some are required to share a cell with one other prisoner. There are also fully adapted cells for residents with disabilities available.

One of the best things I found when I started at Bronzefield was that, unlike Wormwood Scrubs, there is a phone in every resident's room, which they can use once a PIN number is issued soon after arrival. The only place where there is queuing or fighting to use a communal phone is in Reception. The calls are monitored and restricted to certain people, and only have a dial-out option, but at least residents can call home and speak to their families and children when they want to.

The white noise of prison is the sharp jangle of metal on metal, hence the names 'in the can' or 'in the clink'. The clanging as metal doors and gates open and close, keys turn in locks, alarm bells screech if certain gates are not locked within the few seconds allowed. Of course, there is also the sound of women laughing, chattering, shouting, and sometimes screaming, screeching and crying. The rattle of food trolleys as they are pushed to and from the kitchens to the house blocks and back. The crackle of radios butting in, and of people shouting to one another as they run to an emergency somewhere in the prison.

A complete cacophony fills the air.

Chapter Five

'The day I came to prison, I got my life back'

There is such a wide range of diversity in Bronzefield, women of all ages, ethnicities and backgrounds, each with their own unique story. But there are also some common denominators. Many of the women I see in prison are in damaging relationships or have been abused in the past. They may have been abused in childhood, and sadly often repeat the patterns and end up in horrendous abusive relationships, where they are regularly beaten, brutally raped, emotionally abused or stalked. There are strong links between women's experience of abuse and coercive relationships, and reoffending. Many women are inside for supporting their partner's drug use, by shoplifting, selling drugs or committing other offences. It is reported that the majority of women in prison have experienced domestic violence or sexual abuse at some point in their lives, though the true extent of the problem may be even bigger than this. The numbers do not bear thinking about and the stories I hear on a regular basis are deeply shocking and sickening. Despite working there now for four years I have yet to become immune to, or complacent about, the stories I hear. The horrors of what so many women have had to endure is beyond my comprehension. Even though the stories are often similar, and feel almost familiar to me now, each time I hear of the abuse they have suffered it is as if I am hearing it for the first time. I really don't think I will ever come to terms with the thought of what so many of them have been put through.

Abuse, of course, comes in many forms. Sometimes there are women who turn to drugs for comfort and end up homeless and on the streets in awful and desperate situations which are exacerbated by poverty, dependency and poor mental health; sometimes this is not the case. Abuse can also rear its ugly head in places you may not imagine.

*

It was the second time I met Linda that I heard her story. She was a first-timer in her late fifties, who used to be a heavy smoker and suffered with recurrent chest infections

'Hi,' she said, sitting down in front on me, a huge mop of coarse and greying blonde hair framing pale features.

'Hi, Linda. How are you today?'

'I'm not too bad, thanks, Doctor Brown. I've just got a really bad cough again,' she replied, 'and I've been coughing up a load of green muck and wonder if I need some antibiotics. I usually seem to need them when I get like this.'

'Okay, let's have a listen to you.'

I checked the screen was pulled down over the glass opening in the door, and asked Linda to pull up her T-shirt so that I could examine her.

I gently put my stethoscope on her and listened to her chest. There were definitely signs of an infection, so I prescribed her a course of antibiotics.

'Come back and see me again if you don't feel that you are improving, but hopefully the antibiotics will soon start to kick in,' I told her.

'I just want to be well for my son's visit,' she said in a clipped accent, her eyes bright. 'I'm desperate to see him. He's travelling down from Manchester to see me. He's doing a postgraduate degree in computer science. It's been ages since I last saw him. His dad doesn't know that we're in touch. Obviously.'

'Oh?' I replied.

'Yes, that's why I'm here. I tried to cut his penis off with a barbed wire,' she told me matter-of-factly, with a wry expression, the corners of her mouth turned up slightly. 'I didn't manage to finish the job. Sadly.'

Blimey, that's a new one on me, I thought, as I looked at the demure, attractive women sitting in front of me.

I tried to continue the consultation, but it was hard to erase the image of what she had nearly done.

She continued in her bright and cheery way: 'I'm surprised you don't know the story. The girls on the house block think it's brilliant.'

Linda had been married to her husband, Alan, for twenty-eight years.

'We met at work when we were both doing training contracts at the same law firm. I wasn't even looking to date, but he had a knack of saying exactly what I wanted to hear; he convinced me that we wanted the same things out of life and that it was our destiny to be together. He was into huge romantic gestures; once he delivered a single rose every day for a week. On my birthday, there was a red Cartier box on the table and tickets for a surprise weekend trip to Venice. It moved pretty quickly. It was almost too perfect.'

On the strength of their joint salaries, the couple quickly moved in together to a large detached house on the outskirts of one of the local Surrey villages.

'It was a proper, grown-up house, my dream home. It was beautiful, but in the end, it felt like a prison,' she said, shrugging her narrow shoulders and sighing.

Linda and Alan worked hard, drove expensive cars and had three holidays a year.

'To everyone around us, we appeared to have a charmed life. We had everything.

'The control was subtle but was always there, even at the start when I think back. There were red flags everywhere. I knew he was a very angry and jealous person, sometimes he would blow up about a work colleague, or in the car when someone cut him up. One time, when he couldn't switch the TV on in a hotel room, he put his fist through it. Even then, I just silenced my doubts about him. I told myself he was having an off day.

'Mostly, he would chip, chip, chip away at things I said or did, until I felt like I knew nothing. My brain started to feel like a useless grey mush. I ended up relying on what I felt about things less and less, and deferring to him on even the smallest decisions to do with the house.'

'That sounds so dreadful,' I said, trying to imagine how awful it would be to live like that.

'It was.' She raised her eyebrows. 'He questioned me about my every move and monitored all my calls. He made me think I was "going crazy" and went mental when I spoke to any other men, so in the end, I never did. I didn't even make eye contact with another man.'

I recognised these invisible chains of fear I have seen in many women. It can pervade every element of their existence and it is usually so subtle and gradual that it can take over their lives without them realising until it is too late and becomes the norm.

'I started coming home from work earlier and earlier, so he didn't fly off the handle. I avoided any social events and stopped taking on the bigger clients. I would never travel away overnight, but instead would leave at 4 o'clock in the morning if I had to. I was exhausted and started to drop the balls. I started to notice that more junior colleagues were being promoted above me. That just reinforced my feelings that I wasn't good enough.'

Things started to get worse for Linda when she was

pregnant with their first child, a few years after they got married, and Alan's need for control reached new heights.

'He never let me go to any appointments on my own; everything I did, he had to know about. He even made me write lists of what I was eating, as he didn't want me to put on too much weight in my pregnancy, like a food diary. He shouted at me every day about almost everything. He hated the noise I made when I ate, the way I did the shopping was wrong, and he often said that I had spent too much on groceries or I had bought the wrong brand of whatever he wanted. The way I spoke to him wasn't right. It went on and on and on.'

'How awful for you,' I said. 'Are you close to your family? What did they think?'

'He persuaded me that my friends and family were against me,' she replied, looking down at her hands, where I could see she had bitten her nails down to the quick. 'If my mum called, I would have to tell her I was busy. He made me throw away my phone, so I no longer had everyone's numbers. Even now when I think about the things he said and did, I question whether I had provoked him or over-reacted to something he said.'

Linda found joy in her new son but was lonelier than ever. She discovered she was pregnant again just before she returned to work, so she ended up taking more time off than she had intended and then giving birth to a daughter.

'Did you ever go back?' I asked.

'No. I eventually gave up my big job in town after having the kids. He told me I was getting too old, and that they were going to work out a reason to make me redundant and that I should jump first. He let me get a job with a local firm, working alongside two other women.

'It wasn't all bad; we went through periods of time when he would be loving and kind. He would buy me big presents or book a holiday.

'Deep down I always knew that his behaviour wasn't right, but I didn't think I could do anything about it. Or complain. What did I have to complain about?'

However, the aggression always returned and even when she was back at work, life did not improve for Linda.

'As well as working full time, I had to be at home and do everything with the kids. And if dinner wasn't on the table when he returned home, he would go mad. I would rush around every evening, obsessively tidying and cleaning, but it was never good enough.

'He took my salary and gave me an allowance, so I never had the means to do what I wanted. I had to ask him for money to do my hair, or if the children needed new shoes or money for a school trip.

'I don't know what the kids felt, but I wanted to try to keep the peace for their sake, at least. I tried to stay one step ahead of him, but it was almost impossible. I spent the whole time telling them to be good and be quiet, so he wouldn't take it out on them.

'Sometimes he would fly into a rage about something that

had happened several weeks before; I could never predict what would upset him, when and why, however hard I tried.

'He also told me in great detail what would ever happen if I left him. That I would be nothing without him and that I would not be able to function. And that no one would ever put up with me. There was never any respite and I felt small and insignificant.'

The woman who walked into my room didn't seem small or insignificant at all, but it goes to show how, for women like Linda, their confidence can be eroded to the point that their feelings of self-worth reach rock bottom.

'A few times I was late home and he locked me out, so I slept in the garage. Some days he would hide my blue inhaler that I needed if my chest was a bit tight, and he'd laugh watching me race around the bathroom and bedroom frantically opening and closing the drawers feeling like I couldn't breathe.'

'How scary for you. What an evil thing to do.'

I felt for her as I thought about how awful she must've felt, frightened at not being able to breathe properly, the fear and panic most likely making it worse.

Linda also suffered from sexual abuse. 'I could never say no to him, and I never did. I mean, I was his wife.'

Unbeknown to Linda at the time, Alan had been having affairs for many years behind her back and spending a lot of money on prostitutes.

'I first realised what he was doing when we employed a French au pair to help us one summer when the children were young. We had enough space at home for this girl to stay for a few months, to brush up on her English skills. I came home one day to find them both naked in our bedroom. I pretended I didn't see it and hid in the bathroom. I continued as if things were normal, like it was what everyone did with the au pair.'

She sighed heavily, as if defeated.

Then Linda would see signs that he was involved with other women, and realised he had been having affairs since the start of their relationship.

'I would always know when he started seeing someone new. He would start running every weekend or go to the gym more regularly. He would be more irritable than normal, or suddenly overly affectionate. He would stay out late at night. Some nights he didn't even come home and told me he was working away.

'One night about two years ago, I went into his study. I dug around a bit to find his bank statements. He would regularly take out £200, £300, £400, maybe three or four times a month. I knew then that he was using prostitutes. The way he never let go of his phone. Even at night, he would put it next to the bed and then take it with him to the bathroom. Girlfriends, hookers… I know he was stringing them all along.

'One night when the children were with friends, I followed him in the car, to this house in a rough area in a backstreet somewhere.

'In the end I was desperate to leave him, but for the

kids' sake I knew I had to stay until they were at university. Trouble is I just didn't know where to go or how to leave.

'I didn't feel strong enough. I've not been in touch with my two sisters for years, and my parents are old now. I didn't feel I could tell them the truth about Alan.'

She paused and took a deep breath, sitting back in the blue plastic chair opposite me.

'He never hit me or beat me. I almost wish he had. I know it might sound perverse, but at least then there would be signs of how he made me feel, or "evidence".

'I don't even know what really happened that night I attacked him. It was like an elastic band that snapped. I wanted to teach him a lesson and it was the worst thing I could think of.

'We'd both had too much to drink. I'd also taken a sleeping tablet as I've suffered with insomnia for years. The next thing I knew I had some barbed wire from the garage in my hands and he was screaming and there was blood everywhere.

'I called an ambulance and the police. Now I'm here for another year, at least. In a funny way, it's one of the best things I've ever done. The day I came here was the day I got my life back.'

She smiled at me and I couldn't help but return her smile.

Linda and I talked regularly during the time she was inside, whenever she came to see me, and I always enjoyed seeing her.

'I realise what happened to me could happen to any

other woman in a desperate situation. My method was different, but there are other women who have lost it. Do you know Hilda, in House Block Three? We play cards and bingo together sometimes. We told each other our stories and it was basically the same thing. She's 82 and tried to suffocate her husband by putting a pair of his dirty pants in his mouth whilst he was asleep in his chair, and then poured a scalding hot pot of tea on his face.

'She'd lived with him for over fifty years and had finally had enough. We both lived in fear. Hilda says that being in prison has been the best time in her life, and that she'll commit suicide if they try to release her. She's been here for years and genuinely loves it.

'Alan can do what he likes now. The day my divorce came through I ordered extra chocolate on my canteen. Shared it round with some of the other girls. Apparently, he's got a new girlfriend who thinks I'm a psycho. More fool her. My son Jake and daughter Jenny know that's not the case though. I'm very close to them, but I don't want them to know everything; especially about the other women. They still speak to their father, but it's pretty hard for them and they don't know the full story, or at least I hope they don't.'

I felt for Linda and how difficult it must be for her to balance her own emotions against those of her children. I thought about how hard it must have been for her to keep the truth from them.

'Are you attending any group therapy?' I asked. 'There is a lot on offer.'

'I've been working with the mental health team here, and I'm starting to understand what I've been through and that I'm not worthless. My lawyer has told me that I could press charges against him, but I can't face it, or make Jake and Jenny have to go through that. I just want to be free of him.'

Coercive control is now a criminal offence, and this marks a step forward in tackling domestic abuse. In 2015, England and Wales became one of the first nations in the world to criminalise controlling behaviour within relationships, making it punishable by up to five years in prison. Controlling behaviour works to limit women's human rights by depriving them of their liberty and reducing their ability to be responsible for their actions, making them feel controlled, dependent, isolated or scared. Professor Evan Stark, who invented the term, said: 'The victim becomes captive in an unreal world created by the abuser, entrapped by a world of confusion, contradiction, and fear.' I see this in so many of the women I meet.

'Hilda and I, as well as many other women I have met in prison, we understand each other,' Linda told me. 'I've got a job in the call centre working for an outside business in their sales team, and I hope to work for them when I get out.'

I also knew Linda had taken her dedication to helping women a step further, because she was wearing a blue peer worker T-shirt.

'Are you enjoying your peer support work?' I asked.

'Yes, I try to help other women who have gone through

a similar thing to me and suffered, too. Abuse is something that wears people down and control is usually at the heart of it.

'I used to judge people. Now I don't. You never know what someone else is living through.'

How true that is, I thought, realising that that is probably the most powerful lesson I have learned since working in prison.

Chapter Six

'They take you to hell disguised as heaven'

Drugs and prison.

These two words are knotted tightly together. However hard the authorities, government and even prisoners try to unpick them, they remain forever connected.

Many women in Bronzefield are inside because of drug-related offences, including petty theft, shoplifting and burglary. All to fund an addiction. Sometimes women are incarcerated because they are funding a lower-level habit with a bit of dealing to cover their own use. They often end up being a link in the chain of illegal drug supply and fall foul of conspiracy to supply laws. Many are professional people, such as teachers, entrepreneurs, accountants, and estate agents. The skills needed to run a successful drugs supply operation cannot be too far away from those required to run a business.

However, many more prisoners have rampant habits, that have lasted for decades, and they are often in relationships where they are not only co-dependent on each other but co-dependent on drugs and their chemical comforts.

According to the statistics, forty-eight per cent of female prisoners have committed an offence to support someone else's drug use, compared with twenty-two per cent of male prisoners. Thirty-nine per cent of women have a problem with drugs upon arrival at a prison. In my day-to-day work in prison, drug users make up the majority of the women that I see in the clinic.

These women carve out different ways of making money to fund their habits, often turning to prostitution. As one resident explained to me the other day, 'It's easier than shoplifting.' Another commented some time ago, 'I'm a machine and don't feel anything any more.' I don't think I will ever forget the poor bedraggled little soul that uttered those words and how hopeless she looked and sounded.

However, some find their own niche, such as one lady who I have seen return to prison many times. She told me: 'It's all about hotels for me; I get into hotel rooms and nick people's laptops. I don't know how else to survive. It is the only way I know how to earn a living.'

*

I arrived at the prison at 7 a.m., early after a smooth journey. It was a bright autumn morning and I was almost on auto-pilot as I pulled into the road towards the prison, the early sun beaming through my windscreen.

The roads around the prison are normally very quiet at that time of the morning, but on that day, there were six police vans parked along the entrance road of the prison. There were police and sniffer dogs everywhere. I wound down my window.

A policeman looked in.

'Good morning. Are you prison staff?' he asked.

'Yes, I am,' I replied.

'Please can you turn around and park in the visitors' car park?'

I did as I was told and parked up, feeling slightly unnerved and mildly anxious. Prisons are places of routine, and any break to that routine usually means trouble.

I was ushered into the café on the outskirts of the prison site.

The search began.

First, I was asked to place my finger on a machine that detects drugs. As I pressed my finger down, I could feel my heart racing in my chest. Of course, I knew there were no drugs on my hands, but despite that, when I got the all clear, I felt a wave of relief.

I joined the crowd of staff members in the café – a mixture of those arriving to work and those who were leaving after a night shift. We were asked to line up, five in a row.

A sniffer dog was brought along to check us one by one. I had a sandwich in my bag, and I was concerned the dog would detect it. The dog walked around me, sniffing my body, and gently jumped up briefly on his hind legs to reach my face. I didn't feel alarmed, but it was clear that this was a more thorough search than I had had in a long time.

'Thank you, miss,' the officer said, moving on to the next person. 'Can you go through the door on the right?'

We were ushered into another part of the building into individual rooms, where two officers swiped me with a wand and went through my bags and pockets, looking at every single thing in there. I realised with horror how much stuff I had accumulated. As I tipped the contents of my bag out, the two officers laughed at me. I blushed with embarrassment.

'Quite a collection you've got there, miss,' one of them chuckled, as he picked his way through my glasses case, Tupperware lunch box , two stethoscopes, an umbrella, a packet of biscuits, a hair brush, notepad, a three-month-old Sunday supplement, my large coffee mug, blue plastic spoon, a tin of coffee, a tin of powdered milk, and even my own small kettle. For a long time now, I have taken my own kettle into work to save trying to find one to borrow, which was not always easy.

'Are you planning to move in, or will you be going home tonight?' the other officer teased.

In the end, we were all giggling like kids as I shuffled off, clutching my overstuffed bag.

Even though I'd had no reason to worry that morning, it always felt strangely intimidating when these searches took place. But drugs are a huge issue in prison.

I had always been astonished at how drugs get into prison, but I have learned over the years that there are countless ways to do this. As one prisoner told me some years ago, 'As soon as the authorities stop one route, the dealers will find another ingenious way to outsmart them.'

Drugs are thrown over prison walls, dropped by drones, smuggled in babies' nappies, sewn into the hems of clothes. And so it goes on.

Like most things in life, if you want something badly enough, there are means and ways. Spice is sprayed on to letter paper, where it is then cut up into very small pieces and smoked in joints or vapes. In one prison, I heard about a dressing gown that was saturated with spice.

One criminal gang used rats to smuggle drugs into a category C men's prison in Devon. The dead rodents had the items, which included drugs, mobile phones, SIM cards and other contraband, stitched into their stomachs.

There have been reported cases of corrupt officers, and other outside contractors or civilian workers, bringing drugs into the prison from the outside world. The mark-up on these drugs behind bars can be huge. Though I have never seen nor heard of this happening at Bronzefield, and I understand that this is more of an issue in London prisons, everyone knows it happens and it is frequently reported in the national press. Despite the fierce warnings, and signs dotted in the cloakrooms and toilets that staff use to 'not cross the line' and 'you will be caught', in many prisons this practice must continue to be done by a tiny minority, damaging the integrity of the system and the profession. Dealers can make big money on the wings. There is one woman, known to the system, who will try to get herself arrested so she can come into prison and deal drugs inside. Her business is pretty healthy on the outside, but she takes it up at least two gears once inside.

Prisons are doing a lot to try to stamp out drug use, but they are facing an uphill battle and the walls appear to be more porous than ever. In 2017 Bronzefield introduced an ion machine which assists with the detection of new psychoactive substances that have become a major problem in all prisons.

Prison can be a particularly difficult place to be for someone with a drug dependency. For those who are trying to kick a habit, it can be really hard, because in a moment of weakness they may resort to using on the wing, and undo all the progress they have made.

Drugs distort time, and the whole notion of prison is serving time and losing time, so for many, it is a form of self-medication. A way of dealing with loneliness, isolation, shame, trauma, or often very painful memories, and a host of other mental health issues they may be dealing with. In addition, if a prisoner is suffering from severe withdrawal symptoms when they first arrive in prison, they may be tempted to use drugs on top of the methadone they are given. Most of the women tell me it is usually less about getting high or hedonism than blanking out 'the pain in their brain.'

'You can score almost any drug you want on the wing,' one woman told me, but I had no way of knowing if this were true, although I was told when I worked in Wormwood

Scrubs that it was easier to get drugs in prison than it was on the street. Some prisoners conceal their medication to sell on the wing, which makes prescribing safely in prison very difficult. However, if anyone is found concealing the medication they are prescribed, it is stopped immediately. Only recently someone told me that her friend used to conceal part of a tampon in her mouth when she was given her methadone, so that it could soak up as much as possible for her to then sell on the wing. I had heard of men vomiting back their methadone to sell in Wormwood Scrubs, but sucking on a methadone-soaked tampon was a new one for me.

*

When I was first asked to work in the Substance Misuse Clinic, based in House Block One, my heart sank.

House Block One is where most of the substance misusers reside, including many who have just arrived in prison and are suffering badly from withdrawal symptoms, but also those who are trying to detox off methadone. It has a reputation for attracting dealers who can pray on vulnerable residents. It is filled with raw energy, like a fizzy drink can that had been shaken and shaken and could explode at any second.

Until then, my only exposure to substance misusers in Bronzefield had been in Reception on Friday evenings. The women had just arrived in custody and were usually withdrawing. Drug withdrawal is a term to describe a set of symptoms experienced after suddenly stopping chronic use of drugs or alcohol. The body becomes physically dependent, so abruptly stopping usage can make someone very ill. Physical symptoms of this can include nausea and vomiting, diarrhoea, abdominal cramps, headaches, generalised aches and pains, excessive sweating and shivering, goose bumps, runny nose and eyes, and involuntary muscle jerking sometimes referred to as 'body popping'. They can also suffer from depression, anxiety, paranoia, insomnia, panic attacks, short-term memory loss and confusion. The most severe withdrawal symptoms from alcohol, known as delirium tremens, or DT, include elevated body temperature, rapid heart rate, seizures and hallucinations.

Feeling so ill could often make them impatient, rude, abusive, and occasionally aggressive. I sympathised with them – I have seen enough people withdrawing to understand to some extent how dreadful they can feel – but I wasn't sure I wanted to spend my whole working day dealing with such challenging women. But I was persuaded to give it a go – my ultimate and final demon to confront.

My first weeks were a struggle. The room I was allocated to work in was in the centre of house block one in a cramped, windowless room. When I arrived to start the day at about 8 a.m., the residents would all be milling around outside the treatment room, some sitting on the blue plastic chairs waiting for their methadone, and other medication, whilst others would be walking around chatting with each other before they went off to their various daily activities.

It was crowded and usually very noisy, which made even getting into my room a challenge in itself sometimes. I would invariably be confronted by a crowd of women begging to be seen. I could only see the women booked into the clinic, but some of them were so persistent and persuasive that it could be very hard to say no. They were rarely nasty to me, but it was intense, and it was exhausting.

On one of the many difficult days, I had successfully run the gauntlet to my room. Once inside, I locked the door firmly behind me so that I could get on with my work before the clinic was due to start, but often the women would carry on banging and banging on it so much that in the end I usually had to open it as there was no peace until I did. They knew I was in there. There was no hiding place.

I opened the door and three women were stood in front of me, all asking for different things at the same time. I could barely hear what each of them was saying. Very quickly, Shamir, one of the officers, came over.

'Please, ladies, give the doctor some space. If you need to see her there is a proper process. You know you have to have an appointment.'

Reluctantly the women moved away, and I smiled my gratitude to Shamir. I was very grateful in those moments for the staff who arrived at the right time.

The first woman I met that morning was Carol.

'Hi, Doc,' she said, as she sat down, fiddling with her

grey tracksuit that was fraying at the sleeves. 'It's lovely to see you again. I'm only back for a few weeks this time.'

I had seen Carol come in and out of prison many times, but over two years she had managed to finally free herself from her addiction to clonazepam. It was an incredible feat given the depth of her addiction. She had been taking it for twenty-seven years, since she was 17, but somehow on returning to prison she decided enough was enough and that she was going to wean herself off it, even after her release. Despite some lapses along the way she succeeded. Clonazepam belongs to the benzodiazepine family and is still used occasionally to treat epilepsy by preventing and controlling seizures. It was also used to treat anxiety and panic attacks, but it is highly addictive, and prone to abuse. For this reason, it is only rarely prescribed these days.

I thought back to when I had first met her.

She had told me that she had spent most of her childhood in care in Leeds, where she was born. From the age of seven until ten, she was sexually abused, and as an adult she ended up in a series of abusive relationships, in her desperate bid to find love and the family life she had never known.

Carol told me that she used drugs to numb her emotions.

'Pills, drugs, they were my world,' she told me, fiddling with the end of her long straggly hair. 'And I was popping pills for any reason I could think of. If I was in pain, I would pop a pill; if I was sad, I would pop a pill; if I was angry, I would pop a pill; and if I was happy, I would celebrate with pills. Eventually, I relied on pills for everything.'

When she was detained in custody, she had to withdraw from the different drugs she was using, but her biggest struggle was coming off clonazepam.

'Initially I was dragged kicking and screaming off them,' she explained, her hands gesticulating as she spoke. 'It was as though I'd lost a limb – a hand, an arm or leg – or even a best friend. Although it was a downfall of mine a lot of the time, I especially loved the effect of clonazepam and the way it made me feel. Those little white pills, they take you to hell disguised as heaven.'

In prison, all the residents who are addicted to benzos have to detox, and they are given medication to support them. Many of them have been abusing 'benzos' for years, often in very high doses.

They are a hard group of drugs to come off, and frequently the women beg and plead with me to not detox them.

Benzodiazepines are known by various names like 'jellies' and 'eggs' on the street. However, there is a no-tolerance policy of benzos in prison and these women have to go through a detox regime, however hard. They try to appeal to me and talk me round, but I have to give them my little speech about the fact that nobody is maintained on benzos in prison other than a very few people that have them prescribed by the psychiatrist.

I can often see fear, disappointment and sometimes resentment in their eyes when they realise that their crutch is going to be taken away from them.

'The paranoia after coming off them was torture,' said Carol. 'I had no sleep whatsoever. And if I did manage to doze for even a moment or two, I'd have horrible night-mares, which stayed in my mind all day and made me feel even worse.'

I remembered seeing her during this period, and like many of the other prisoners withdrawing from drugs, how sad and unwell she looked. She had a haunted look with empty vacant eyes and a flat expression. As if she wasn't quite with it.

'I remember how much you struggled and how very unwell you were,' I said.

'It was awful. I had other strange withdrawal symptoms. I had cramps, spasms, seizures, and even went blind for a bit, which was very scary. I've no idea why this happened but it was probably due to my body going without the chemicals it had come to rely on,' she said. 'For a while, I could only make out shapes, colours and blurred images in the distance.' Carol had partnered up with another resident inside, another common occurrence in women's prisons, where many women sought out same-sex relationships with other inmates for intimacy and support.

'My ex had to do everything for me; she even had to read and write for me. I forgot who I was and even though she's my ex now, I'm grateful for her support. I lost myself.

'It was hell. It took sixteen months before I got a decent night's sleep. My anxiety was through the roof. I've tried to withdraw from them so many times before, but just kept failing. For me, I reckon that every year I was on benzos added another month to the withdrawal process. I also reckon that the older you are, the more awful it is,' she said.

On one occasion shortly after her release from prison, Carol was admitted to a psychiatric hospital under the Mental Health Act as she was in such a mess.

'Three days after my release, I was sectioned. It was like my brain had been cracked open and fried, like an egg.

'The maddest thing of all? I was still desperate for this drug. Even though it caused me all this pain and torment in the first place, it didn't stop me wanting one last pill. I found it impossible to focus on anything else for a year and a half.'

Not long after, she was back in prison, but continued to withdraw from the drug that had blighted her life.

She said she now looked back through the 'benzo fog of withdrawal' with complete clarity.

'It was a shock to the system but also amazing. Even though things looked strange, they were beautiful. My senses were reawakened. Colours and smells were all so clear and pure. Even textures I hadn't felt since I was a child, felt new and brilliant.

'After trudging uphill for so long, I have finally levelled out and found myself again.'

'I can't believe how you've managed to get through this, Carol,' I told her. 'It's an incredible achievement – you have done unbelievably well.'

'Thanks, Doc. I reckon I owe you and some of the other people here my life.'

For Carol, her life was finally easier and not solely about drugs. 'Now, over two years later, I can sleep, eat and think, without those little white pills. I lost a huge part of my adult life to them. If you think benzo withdrawal will never end, it only seems that way. If you'd told me, two years ago, I'd be free from that drug, I would not have believed you. But now? I'm living the dream.

'I know that may sound daft as I am back in prison again, but it's only for a few weeks on licence recall, and then I should be done with prison.'

She smiled, adding, 'It's about time! Thank God I no longer need to commit crime to pay for my habit.

'Also, I managed to get a qualification last time I was in here, and I'm in touch with a charity that helps women find a job after release from prison. So, I feel really hopeful and positive, finally, about my future.'

She sat quietly for a moment reflecting on her story, while I found it really wonderful to hear a happy ending for a change. So often I hear of hopelessness and despair, so it made me feel good too, to know that sometimes, just sometimes, people can take back control of their lives and find happiness.

I hugged her and wished her luck. As we said goodbye, I had a feeling that I would most likely never see her again, which was strangely bittersweet.

What I found incredible was that, invariably, once these women had withdrawn from alcohol and/or the variety of drugs they may have been using and were stable, by far the majority were lovely people, albeit many of them were also very damaged. Some of the women took a long time to trust me but once they did, I learnt far more about the physical and emotional issues around their drug and alcohol dependency. Even though I am a doctor, and have now dealt with hundreds of people in the Substance Misuse Clinic, the truth is that I will never really understand their dependencies in the way that they do.

It is a complex and individual experience, and can depend on many different factors, including how long someone has been struggling with an addiction, the types of drugs they are addicted to, how much of the drug they have been using, the method they use to take it and, importantly, their mental and physical health.

At any one time, a third of the prisoners inside Bronzefield are there for three weeks or less, many of them detained for theft offences. HMP Holloway, previously the largest women's prison in Western Europe and the only women's prison in London, closed in 2016. The women were moved to Bronzefield and to other women's prisons. HMP Downview, a prison in Surrey that had lain vacant for two years, was reopened to take prisoners for whom spaces elsewhere could not be found. The impact of Holloway's closure was felt across the country and Bronzefield reportedly now receives 200 additional women every quarter. This very high turnover of prisoners is not just problematic from an organisational perspective of trying to cope with a much less stable and settled population, but dealing with medical and mental health issues, and managing withdrawal from drugs and alcohol, can also be very difficult and much riskier with a short sentence. Some women tell me that they ask the judge for a long enough sentence to get the help they need.

I see many women who are addicted to a variety of drugs and alcohol, including heroin, and the majority of them are also homeless; they may lose their housing as a result of being sent to prison, or may simply have never been able to access housing in the first place. The vast majority of these women have no 'fixed abode', as well as a drug habit to contend with. Some manage to maintain on a methadone or buprenorphine script in the community to try to help them 'stay clean' and aid their recovery, but often they will use heroin on top of the methadone script, and end up with an even bigger habit. Some of them tell me that if they are not on a methadone script they buy it, as it is cheaper than heroin.

I hate with a passion the way illegal drugs, and heroin use in particular, can destroy lives. I have heard time and time again of how people I meet in prison have lost everything as a result of their addiction, and how they long to get their lives back and be drug free. It is evil in my view. Logic dictates that if something is bad for you, you stop doing it, but when heroin is in the picture, there seems to be no logic.

Cherelle was a resident I knew well and was someone who described her road into addiction clearly. I saw her many times over the eighteen months that my clinic was on House Block One. One day she came in to see me and started to open up more about her life and her path into drugs. In her mid-forties, she had been in and out of prison more than twenty times and had started using drugs when she was 14. On the outside, she had a series of abusive boyfriends, who also had their own drug addictions.

Physically, she looked at least twenty years older than she was, and had tugged and pulled her hair so much that her dreadlocks were interspersed with bald patches. Her dark eyes were bloodshot with dark circles ringing them, and her skin was flaky and dry. Her arms were covered with track marks and small scabs which she told me were the result of her constantly picking at her skin. She looked so run down, and had a large cold sore on her lower lip that she said had appeared five days ago, so it was too late to respond to treatment. It just had to run its painful course. Over the time I had seen her in and out of the prison, she had continued to lose more and more weight, and was looking thinner than ever.

Her tracksuit hung off her like a sack.

'How are you feeling?' I asked her.

'I know for some people prison is the worst thing that might ever happen to them,' she told me. 'But for me, every time I'm sentenced, I just feel so relieved. On the outside I've been shouted at, bullied and assaulted, so being inside here is a piece of cake. It's my happy place. I'm never sure what day it is, or what month it is, so it suits me here. Every day is the same.'

Cherelle grew up in South London. She was the youngest

of four sisters and her dad was in and out of prison for theft, burglary and violence throughout her childhood. The other children at her local primary school would surround her, chanting, 'Where's your father gone? Where's your father gone?'

Her dad eventually died in prison from a drug overdose when she was just 10. The authorities said they couldn't be sure if it was accidental, but she was told one day he wasn't coming home, and that was it.

'My one aim in life is to not die in prison,' she told me. 'I do want to live a normal, regular life on the outside, I just don't know how to do it. I'd love more than anything to be clean.'

'I've heard so many other women say the same thing to me, Cherelle,' I told her. 'If you really want to, I'm sure you can get there.'

'I want it more than anything,' she said.

Cherelle's sisters moved out as soon as they could and went on to live their own messy lives, whilst her mother struggled with her drug habit, taking casual work as and when she could. The rest of the time she would sit around their flat with her mates 'shooting up'. When Cherelle returned from school, she would often find them slumped across the worn-out sofas and find more cigarette burns on the threadbare carpet.

'I still don't understand why I wasn't taken into care,' she said. 'I know Mum wanted the best for me, and sometimes she was okay. But most of the time, she wasn't. I feel guilty saying it, but sometimes I wish I had been adopted. I think I would have had a better life.'

As a young teen, she started bunking off school, drinking and taking drugs with some other kids on the estate.

'Then I met a bloke who was fifteen years older than me, and he got me onto heroin. Looking back, that was the beginning of the end of my life. It was cheaper than cocaine and alcohol then.

'The first time I tried it, I was 14. I remember it so well. It was instantly fucking amazing. I felt so safe and warm. It lasted about five hours. I'd never felt anything like it before. It was like everything was melting and nothing mattered any more. Like I was being wrapped up in a warm blanket. I decided that this was going to be my life. I was hooked.'

Then her life started to unravel.

'I lied to myself, lied to my friends, lied to everyone. Nothing else mattered. I didn't give a fuck about anything or anyone. It became my whole world and all I thought about.'

Cherelle went from smoking heroin to injecting it to get the 'rush'. But as with most heroin addicts, Cherelle had to score more and more heroin and take it in higher doses to get the same effect.

'But eventually, there's no longer that feeling of euphoria,' she said. 'I just needed a bigger and bigger hit to stop feeling like shit. I injected in my arms, groin, feet, hands, neck, wherever I could, until in the end there was nowhere left to inject as all my veins were too hard. I'm amazed I never got a blood clot or serious infection, like so many of my mates did. I suppose I should be grateful for that at least,' she said with a little smile.

'My dealers would serve me up two and two and it was gone in no time.'

'What does two and two mean?' I asked.

'Two bags of heroin and two bags of cocaine. It was costing me so much in the end I had to resort to sex work, which was really scary. A couple of times I was beaten up when they'd finished with me. It is something I never thought I'd end up doing.

'I never thought I could reach such depths of despair and sink so low.

'Drugs to me were like emotional anaesthesia, but when they wore off hell returned with a vengeance.

'Now I wonder how £10 got me high. I just needed to score to stop the terrible withdrawal symptoms taking hold. You feel like you're gonna die when you're clucking, believe me.'

She looked so small and sad, and I felt frustrated that despite all her stints in prison, she had never successfully managed to kick her habit and get clean, even though she had tried countless times.

'I've lost count of the times I've tried to give up, and each time I try I fail. Guess what I do when I think I've failed? Take more heroin.'

Initially, when they come into custody, women addicted to heroin can only be given a small dose of 10ml of methadone, but this is gradually increased for most people over the next few days to 30 or 40ml, until their symptoms of opiate withdrawal are controlled, although it can sometimes take up to seven days to stabilise on a dose.

Most of the new arrivals will already be in the process of withdrawing, and are occasionally faecally incontinent as the diarrhoea they get can be so bad that they say they 'could shit through the eye of a needle.' Sometimes they vomit in the sweatbox – the van that brings them into prison from the courts – and they have to be taken to the showers as soon as possible after they arrive.

When they are reviewed over the next few days the dose of methadone may need to be 'titrated up', to enable them to stabilise. When they are not stable, they usually feel really dreadful and if they have a big habit on the outside they may need a dose of 60ml to 80ml before they feel comfortable. When I see them in the clinic quite often they will say that the dose they are on is just not holding them through twenty-four hours, and that 'By 4 a.m. I'm clucking me tits off, Doc. 30ml is nowhere near enough.'

Titrating up to the correct dose of methadone needs to be carefully managed. If someone is only inside for a few weeks, it is often safer to maintain them on a higher dose, so that they are at less risk of overdose and possibly killing themselves when they are released. Also, if they are on a methadone script there is a chance that they will stay on a script and not go back to using heroin. This is what a lot of people have told me. Sadly so often, and for all sorts of reasons, many of them do not last very long on a script and fall back into their old ways.

On the other hand, if someone has received a long enough sentence to get help, very often they will ask to titrate up to a dose that stabilises them, and when they feel totally comfortable will come back to see me to discuss and plan their detox, often presenting me with their detailed plans as to how quickly or slowly they want to do it.

Some people refer to methadone as 'liquid handcuffs', as they cannot cope without it and have to attend a clinic or chemist every day to take a supervised dose if they are on a maintenance script outside. 'Normal' activities like holidays or even nights away can be impossible, as if they don't attend to take their methadone they will feel unwell, and if they do not attend for more than a few consecutive days they may not be allowed to stay under the clinic's care. These women are living it and I have to respect the way they want to manage it.

Cherelle had been diagnosed with bipolar disorder, and had an extensive history of self-harm, and so had spent a lot of time located in the Healthcare wing when she was in prison.

That day, I was checking that her dose of methadone was adequate and she was comfortable.

'Is it enough to hold you through twenty-four hours?' I asked.

'Yeah, it's fine thanks, Doc. I don't want to be on more than I need to be 'cos I want to start a detox when I feel ready,' she replied. 'Can I come back and see you when I feel strong enough to do it?'

'Of course, you can,' I replied. I knew how hard and scary the process of detox could be, as many women told me they were frightened to come off drugs because they would have to confront their true emotions and the horrors of their past.

Every time I saw Cherelle arrive back in custody, I hoped that this time might be the one stay that would change things for her, and that just maybe she would never return.

*

Quite often the residents present with complications resulting from their drug use, one of the most common being skin infections. This is due not only to the drugs themselves and their impurities, but the way they are delivered, such as intravenously. Also, the unhealthy lifestyles associated with drug use, such as poor nutrition and lack of sufficient sleep. One lady, called Jessica, arrived in the clinic having only been in prison for a few days, and looked so sad and run down in her grey prison tracksuit. She was in her forties but looked a lot older, with sunken cheeks and hollow eyes. She was unkempt and it looked as if the years of drug use had taken their toll.

'Hi Jessica. How are you? What can I do for you today?'

'My hand is killing me,' she said. 'The pain kept me awake all night. It's unbearable now.'

'How long has it been hurting? Can I have a look?'

'It's got worse over the past two days but now it's really

throbbing,' she replied, showing me her hand. She had a really large red swelling on the back of her hand.

'That's a really nasty abscess. Have you been injecting there?'

'Yeah. I'm so stupid for doing it but I just can't stop myself.'

Thankfully, I am not squeamish at all about dealing with a festering abscess. In fact, I find it totally gratifying to perform incision and drainage of a big bag of pus. It is so satisfying, and the relief for the patient is really wonderful. Very many years ago when I worked in A&E I earned the nickname of 'Pus Ball Brown', as everyone I worked with knew how excited I got at the thought of draining an abscess. So, I am more than happy to oblige if someone presents with an abscess caused by injecting.

'Would you like me to try and drain this for you?' I asked. 'It will relieve the pain and make your hand feel much more comfortable.'

'Yes, please,' she told me. 'Anything you can do to make it less painful.'

It only needed a tiny incision to let a vast quantity of pus pour out. It was incredible, and the relief for her was immediate.

'You're really enjoying this, aren't you?' she smiled.

'Yes, I find it so satisfying,' I said.

I could not hide the obvious joy I got from seeing all the pus drain away, and she in turn could not help but smile, and we ended up having a really good laugh about my strange fascination with pus.

'I've never met anyone quite as weird as you, Doctor Brown,' she laughed. 'Most people throw up when they see pus like that.'

It was a win-win for both of us, and so lovely to see someone that had walked into my room looking so miserable, walk out looking so much happier. Simple pleasures cheer my day.

*

Sometimes medical issues relating to drug use can be far more serious. Anna was a woman I knew well from her frequent visits to prison. On one particular occasion when she returned, I saw her at the end of my shift in Reception just before 9 p.m.

When she came into my room, she looked pale and totally exhausted. She promptly slumped down in the chair as soon as she could. She told me that she had pain in her right groin which made it uncomfortable to walk.

She had been in police custody for the two nights before arriving back at Bronzefield.

'The Old Bill took me down to A&E two nights ago 'cos it was so bad,' she said, 'but the doctor I saw just said I'd sprained a ligament. I don't believe him though 'cos I don't think I've sprained anything.

'They was so busy down there, the poor bloke didn't know if he was coming or going. I almost felt sorry for the poor bastard. Also, I was cuffed up, and I think he wanted to get rid of me as quick as he could.'

Anna was withdrawing badly from heroin, but despite feeling so ill she was her usual polite and friendly self with me. She was in her late thirties and had been injecting heroin for years.

I checked her groin and found that she had a very small swelling that was a bit red and tender. It seemed almost insignificant, and I thought it unlikely that it could be the cause of so much discomfort.

However, I thought it best to start her on antibiotics as a precaution as clinically I suspected it may be a small abscess starting to develop.

'I'm going to start you on some antibiotics,' I told her, 'to be on the safe side. Is that okay with you?'

She agreed to this, and after sorting out all the other medication she needed she headed off to the house block to get her head down, while I headed home to do the same.

When I came to work two days later, I was told that Anna had deteriorated rapidly and had been rushed to hospital on Saturday afternoon with sepsis, and that she had to have extensive emergency surgery to try to save her leg. The infection had spread down into her leg and caused necrotising fasciitis. In all the forty years since qualifying, I had never come across this before. Sometimes referred to as the 'flesh-eating disease', bacteria release toxins that damages the surrounding tissues, and what starts as a small injury or infection can in extreme cases become life-threatening.

Anna spent five weeks in hospital undergoing a series of operations in a bid to save her from amputation. She was incredibly lucky that the surgeons managed to save her leg. I must admit that I felt very relieved that I had at least started her on antibiotics, as I would have felt dreadful if I hadn't and the end result had turned out differently. I almost couldn't bear to think of it.

When I saw her back in prison, she told me what had happened.

'It burst almost as soon as I got to hospital, and it was pissing pus everywhere! I was so embarrassed, and the smell was evil.

'It was just pouring down me leg, as if I'd pissed meself!' she said laughing.

She had fully recovered, and regained her lovely sense of humour. She proceeded to show me the extensive scars on her groin and down her leg. The wounds had healed beautifully and were really neat.

'The surgeons and all the doctors and nurses were totally awesome! I cannot tell you how grateful I am to them. I am NEVER going to inject again,' she said. I hoped that she would stick to her pledge.

*

One morning a nurse asked me to see a 37-year-old lady called Farzana who had arrived in custody three days previously. She was really unwell from opiate withdrawal, and was desperate for as much methadone as possible, but as usual it had to be titrated up from 10ml on day one, 20ml on day two and 30ml by day three. However, the nurses did not feel happy to give her methadone that morning because her pulse and blood pressure were so low that it would have been unsafe to give her any at all, let alone a little more. When she was told that she could not have her methadone, she became very angry, demanding and abusive to the nurse, and so an instant message popped on to my computer screen asking me to see her in the clinic to decide how best to proceed. I was really not looking forward to seeing her, as it would be most unlikely that she would be able to have any methadone, and so I was pretty sure that I would be next in the firing line of her anger when I had to inform her of this. I had never met her before, and I could feel my anxiety levels rise in anticipation.

As soon as she came into my room she flopped onto the chair, crossed her arms on my desk and lay her head on them.

She was skeletally thin, pale and unkempt and was too exhausted to speak initially, so she just sat there for a few moments, until eventually she looked up at me with sunken eyes.

'Do you mind if I lie down?' she said, turning her gaze to the couch in my little room. 'I feel like shit.'

Together with the Healthcare Assistant who was working with me, we helped her to her feet and onto the couch where she lay on her side in the foetal position clutching her stomach.

She was excessively drowsy, and her pulse and blood

pressure were extremely low, which was unusual as normally the heart rate and blood pressure go up when someone withdraws from opiates, so the picture was not making sense clinically.

For a moment she opened her eyes and uttered, 'Please, please give me my methadone. I feel so ill. I just can't cope with this.'

I was very wary about the reaction my reply would cause.

I told her: 'I am so sorry, but it would be far too dangerous to have methadone right now. Have you used anything on the wing that may have made you so drowsy and made your pulse and blood pressure so low?'

I dreaded the anger that this question might induce.

'No, nothing. I just need my meth,' she whispered quietly.

She was not rude or angry with me to my relief and surprise.

I stood by her side and put my hand on her shoulder saying nothing for a few minutes as she closed her eyes again and we shared the silence.

I gently then explained that she was far too unwell to be in prison and needed to be admitted to hospital.

She stayed in for ten days, and when I saw her again a few weeks later she was so apologetic.

'I feel so bad for causing so much trouble,' she said. 'I know you did the right thing. I think it saved my life going to hospital. I also feel really bad that I didn't tell you the truth, as actually I was using loads of spice before I came to prison, and I came in with some in my moo moo, so I could carry on using it in prison.'

How many times have I heard that before, I thought.

'I've become so addicted to it, even though sometimes it makes me feel like shit. It's as if I'm in another reality, like I'm in a computer game when I use it. It's hard to describe, exactly,' she went on to explain.

Spice has infiltrated Bronzefield, and I suspect has probably found its way into most other prisons as well. It was the reason I finally gave up working in Wormwood Scrubs and I hope it won't defeat me again in Bronzefield, although there are times when I think it will. It is a synthetic cannabinoid made up of a mixture of chemicals, sometimes including traces of heavy metals, which makes it even more dangerous.

It is far more vicious unpredictable and powerful than the natural form of cannabis.

Residents very often end up in Separation and Care (referred to as 'The Seg' in most other prisons) – a separate unit where prisoners get sent as a punishment, or for their own protection, as a result of using spice, because it can make them behave in such a bizarre way, often becoming violent, aggressive and abusive.

When it first came onto the drug scene it was legal and not thought to be addictive, but this is not the case, as it has proved to be highly addictive and its effects can last for a long time. This is due to the fact that it bonds strongly to the receptors in the brain, and repeated use causes a build-up of the drug, making the effect much more powerful.

It can cause hallucinations, paranoia, seizures, rigidity,

chest pain, difficulty breathing, abdominal cramps, vomiting, headaches, and altered perception. In addition, it can cause reduced blood flow to the heart that can lead to a heart attack, and death. Other effects on the cardiovascular system include slowing or conversely speeding up the heart rate and raising or lowering blood pressure. It seems extraordinary that the effects are so variable, but it is because of the variation of extra ingredients it can contain, including rat poison.

I thanked her for telling me the truth, as I needed to understand why she had been in such a dreadful state. She had almost certainly had such a build-up of the drug in her body that it had caused her pulse and blood pressure to be very low.

'I must admit that you scared me. You were in a right mess,' I said smiling back at her.

She looked at me for a little while and then continued: 'I have a real problem trusting anyone, especially doctors, but I feel I can trust you, which is a first.'

It was another moment to treasure in an otherwise bonkers world.

*

When my morning clinic on House Block One was over I would always wait until the noise outside died down, because I knew then that everyone should be locked up and that it would be safe to go across to the loo on the opposite side of the atrium, hopefully without anyone having a go at me. I snuck out, locked the door, and walked across to the loo, only to find four residents waiting by the gate. They were due to go back to work in the call centre and needed an officer to open up and let them out.

On that particular day as I was unlocking the door of the staff loo just by the gate, one of them came over and started shouting at me, and pointing her finger at my face, so close I thought she was going to poke my eye out.

She was angry about her pregabalin, and even though it was nothing to do with me, as another doctor was dealing with it, she had a right go at me.

Lucy was in her late-thirties and was tall and solid, with an extremely loud voice. She was definitely the kind of person you would want on your side if a fight broke out.

'Doctor Brown, you didn't get my meds sorted out. It's disgraceful. My solicitor is gonna be dealing with this. You're crap at your job. You said you'd booked me a GP appointment and you didn't. I still ain't been seen, and I'm really struggling without me pregabs.'

She was so close to me that her spit sprayed across my face. Her breath was warm and sour.

I was furious, and my heart started to race so fast I thought I was going to explode. I was shaking with rage. It was so unlike me to rise to the bait, but I just couldn't help myself.

'Don't you *dare* point at me and speak to me like that. I have sorted it out for you and I really don't appreciate you having a go at me,' I snapped back.

I was boiling inside and must have looked so angry that she was taken aback.

I don't think anyone has seen me lose it at work before, but I certainly did that day. I am definitely not proud of allowing myself to show how angry I was.

Luckily the other three women came over and told Lucy to leave me alone.

It was the final straw.

In total, I had managed to survive eighteen months working on House Block One. But that day, I decided that if I could not even go to the loo in peace in my lunch hour, enough was enough. From then on the Substance Misuse Clinic moved back to the Healthcare department and I continued my clinics from there.

*

Sometime after that horrible incident, Lucy returned to prison again one Friday night when I was working in Reception, and so I knew I had to see her.

I was dreading it, but I had no choice. I had to confront her, but to my massive relief she apologised to me, which was so wonderful.

As she walked into my room her arms were open and she looked me straight in the eye.

'I am so sorry for what happened,' she said. 'I shouldn't have treated you like that.' And with that she gave me a hug.

She was like a different person, as she had managed to get off her drugs and was feeling wonderful.

'I'm done with drugs. I'm just back on twenty-eight-day recall and then it's over. No more prison. I've even managed to get housed and get a job, so life is worth living again. I have a future to look forward to at long last.'

Her face was clearer, and her eyes were brighter, and she was hardly recognisable from the angry person I knew before.

'I'm sorry too,' I said. 'It was unlike me to behave like that and I felt dreadful afterwards.'

I really hate falling out with people, and can count on one hand the women I've fallen out with at Bronzefield, and without exception, they have all apologised for their behaviour and we have made our peace.

That's the magic to me; I will forgive anyone for just about anything. It was a special moment. In the main, I try never to judge the people I meet in prison for what has gone before. I start with a blank slate and we build our own relationships.

Chapter Seven

**'I put myself back together bit by bit like a
jigsaw puzzle, and slowly that dark tunnel
that was my sentence had glimmers of light'**

The applause that rang out as the cast took their bows
to a standing ovation was almost deafening. I had just
finished watching the most fantastic performance of *Sweet
Charity*. There were sparkling costumes, an incredible set,
and a twelve-piece orchestra belting out the show's tunes,
like 'Big Spender' and 'If My Friends Could See Me Now'.

But this was no West End show; I was firmly rooted to the
slightly sticky floor of the gym at Bronzefield. Featuring an
Olivier-nominated actress and other professionals, the show
was put on by The Pimlico Opera, a charity that produces
performances in prisons and primary schools.

There was a singer-songwriter, a busker and an opera-
trained singer among Bronzefield's residents, all of who
couldn't wait to get on stage, but many of the others had
never acted before, or even been to the theatre. Other residents worked backstage on jobs like lighting and set design.

At one point during the show, it was quite hard to tell

the difference between the amateurs and the professionals. The singing was fantastic, and at some of the solos I felt myself getting quite emotional.

Seeing the faces of the residents on stage as they welcomed the applause, I could see how much the experience had meant to them. It must have offered them a large boost of self-esteem and a truly wonderful experience of working in a team. As I left the gym that night, I was proud of them.

This is just one example of the ways prison can try to rehabilitate prisoners. Whilst it is right prisoners take responsibility for their actions and the crimes they have committed, this is only part of the story. By developing the residents' education and employment prospects, this hopefully gives them a better chance of finding a new life away from crime on the outside. Hopefully, what it can do is open them up to opportunities and increase their awareness of what they could do, and how they could change.

Many residents end up in prison due to their lack of education. According to the Prisoners' Education Trust who do amazing work, thirty-one per cent of female prisoners have been expelled or permanently excluded from school. The same number have also been taken into care as children, so may have had long periods of time away from the classroom, or moved home and school, with all the emotions that that may have brought with it. Some kids simply slip out of the system. One girl told me: 'I cared for my mum who was ill. We moved around a lot and she died when

I was 14. After that, I just hung out with my friends and ended up getting involved in some bad stuff.'

Just under half of all people entering prison do not have any qualifications at all, so many of them may simply not have the skills to perform meaningful work or be able to provide for themselves or their families.

With employment playing a key role in reducing reoffending, prison provides them with learning opportunities so they can take more responsibility for rehabilitation and unlock their own potential. But fear can stop many of the women seeking help: fear of change, of feeling different, or of being mocked or 'being told I am thick; it would take me right back to being at school, when nobody understood me or what I needed.'

When women enter prison, they sit basic maths and English tests during their induction period, to determine whether they go into education or work. The process at Bronzefield is called Next Steps. While they used to be assessed on their second day of prison, when they may not be in any fit state mentally or physically to sit a test, the process now takes place over a week or so and gives them a chance to acclimatise. They also learn about stress relief techniques, relaxation and healthy living, and how to set short- and long-term goals. This means that even those women who are locked up for just a few weeks, or even days, can take something beneficial from the process.

Many women have undiagnosed learning disabilities and learning difficulties and are assessed carefully during induction to ensure their needs can be met. Some of them may not be able to tell the time, or understand simple instructions, so are not only lost outside the prison system but may end up getting into trouble in prison for uncooperative behaviour, maybe even ending up in Separation and Care if their problems are not recognised.

'I didn't fit in at a normal school, so they sent me to a special school, and I didn't fit in there either. There wasn't enough help and when I left, I couldn't get a job, so crime seemed like the easiest option,' one woman told me. 'I just say yes to everything. Sometimes they tell me two things at once, so I just say yes, I don't want anyone to think I'm thick. Sometimes it's as if I can't explain myself.'

Many women coming into prison have limited ability to read and write, so they are deemed at a 'pre-entry level', so not at the level they need to be to access the normal educational classes. They often feel vulnerable, isolated and embarrassed. They may not even admit they have a problem, but are unable to read letters from home, official documents, or use the pod system, the electronic kiosk system that the women use to order their canteen and make appointments. One woman who was learning to read and write told me that her aim was simply to be able to read her daughter a bedtime story when she left prison.

Often when I walk to my clinic in Healthcare through Main Street, I see women rushing to their classes and work placements. Non-English speaking residents can take English language courses. More educated prisoners can work towards formal City & Guilds qualifications, or apply to do a range of distance learning courses, such as Open University courses, with funding from the Prisoners' Education Trust. There are also links and partnerships with local universities, and there is even a group of criminology students who come into the prison to learn alongside residents, with a scheme called Learning Together. I have heard that the impact on everyone involved is profound. I see the recognisable peer support and Listeners in their bright T-shirts, as well as volunteers from charities such as The Shannon Trust, who help to inspire and help prisoners learn to read. It is incredible to see the impact that simple things, like being able to read, or making a card, can have on women's self-esteem, and the change in some women between when they arrive in prison and when they leave.

Alongside formal learning, women can also move into vocational education, including hairdressing, catering and hospitality, business administration, food hygiene, cleaning or barista training. I think the variety of opportunities that the women have at Bronzefield is wonderful. There is a large hair and beauty salon, called Shades of Beauty, which is kitted out with industry-standard equipment, such as massage beds and hairdressing basins, where prisoners and staff can get their hair cut and coloured, or have beauty treatments from other residents. There is the art-led centre called Jailbirds, where the women create and make art and items such as cards and jewellery, which are then sold through head office, to other residents via the pod system, and at local craft fairs. Women's work is often entered into the Koestler Awards, which runs across different categories such as fine art, craft and design, writing, and film and animation. This is a prison arts charity, that encourages people in the criminal justice system to change their lives by participating in the arts, and residents regularly pick up top awards for their work.

Prisoners working at the café, call centre and salon sign a contract of employment to complete training and commit to stay for a minimum of four months to mimic work outside.

Women also work across many areas of the prison, including in the café, the garden, the kitchens, laundry, servery, Reception and gym. They also work as cleaners covering different parts of the prison, this includes bio-hazard cleaning. There is also a small group of women doing routine maintenance work, including decorating and woodwork. Some work as peer supporters; this refers to a wide range of activities where residents help others, in learning, mentoring or providing practical assistance for anyone with a disability. Occasionally they may also act as advocates for someone lacking the confidence to speak up for themselves.

Last but not least by any means, there are the women who work as Listeners, trained by the Samaritans, who provide confidential emotional support to their fellow inmates who are struggling to cope. The aim is to have enough Listeners available around the clock, for anyone who needs them – a lifeline for those who are feeling depressed, lonely, or even suicidal. Being a Listener is an unpaid role but a very important and unique one. As Amber, who I worked with in Reception, once said to me: 'Being a Listener is an opportunity for me to give something back. I want to help others.'

There really is a whole myriad of things women can do inside if they wish to use the opportunities available. For many inmates, to be given the chance to learn again or be given an opportunity to learn a skill can be life-changing.

There are also two cafés run by prisoners, one inside and one just outside in the prison grounds, The Community Coffee Shop. The café in the prison, Vita Nova, employs twelve women, and a lot of the staff, myself included, eat there when they can. The food is excellent.

As I entered the café one lunchtime, one of the officers told me that there was a freeze on movement.

A roll count is done three times a day to check prisoner numbers, and if it is not correct residents can't move until everyone is accounted for. Chances were that the start of my clinic would be delayed, so I decided to eat there instead of taking the food back to my room.

As I queued for my coffee and panini, I reflected on my morning. I had seen lots of different problems, including one lady in her late seventies who was locked up for arson. I couldn't get her out of my mind. She had very complex mental health issues, and an extensive history of self-harm going back many years. She certainly needed to be in a secure environment, but I really wondered whether prison was the best place for someone with such far-reaching needs.

There are a significant number of residents in Bronzefield over the age of 70, and the numbers continue to rise. Many of these convictions are for women inside for the first time. Understandably, many struggle with issues related to their age, including mobility problems, dementia and incontinence. There are popular focus groups aimed at this age range, such as bingo, crochet, card-making and age-related healthcare talks. The cut-off age for work at Bronzefield is the retirement age, so if residents choose to, they can give up work and receive 'retirement pay'.

The lady I had seen earlier in the day was frail and slightly confused. She appeared to be struggling to cope with prison rules and regulations, having only recently arrived in custody. She did not appear to be able to grasp quite why she was there, and kept asking me to let her go home. I know that she had committed a crime, but it was just so sad.

I have met other people detained in custody with obvious learning difficulties, and I sometimes try to imagine how they process the reality of where they are. One young girl with a chromosomal abnormality just could not understand what was going on and was so distressed. She kept asking me to let her go home to see her dog. She asked me over and over again, and was unable to comprehend my answer when I told her that I did not have the power to do such a thing. It is heartbreaking and feels so cruel when someone does not understand the reality of their situation.

One of the residents brought my food and coffee over to my table.

'It's been so busy this morning,' she said. 'There was a forum here – something important – and loads of business-men and women arrived. We did all the teas, coffees, and sandwiches. I'm knackered.'

'I bet you are,' I replied. 'But you all do a great job in here, the food's really good.'

'Thanks! It's hard work, but good fun really. I'm glad I've finished my shift though. I'm ready to sit down. My legs are aching like fuck.' She laughed. 'But we can't go back to the house block yet because of the freeze on movement.'

'Why don't you sit down and join me for a minute?' I suggested.

She pulled up a chair and sat down heavily, relieved to have a rest.

'I like your perfume,' she said.

When I told her it was called 'Escape' she laughed.

'That's a great name for a perfume to wear in prison.'

'I know,' I said, always childishly pleased when anyone asked what it was called.

'It smells lovely. Are you one of the directors?'

'No, I'm one of the doctors here,' I said. 'Do you get a few hours off after your shift?'

'Nope, I've got education classes later, but I really enjoy them.'

Chelsea started to tell me more about herself. She had been a sickly child and had missed quite a lot of school, and was also dyslexic, something that was only recognised when she had entered prison, two years previously.

'I found that the more school I missed, the more difficult it was to ever catch up, so I was always behind and I had no confidence at all. It was awful. People used to tease me and make fun of me. None of the teachers really knew what to do with me, so I left school when I was 15 and didn't have any qualifications.

'Around then, I met my daughter's dad, who was a lot older than me, and life descended into chaos. He started to abuse me, and so I started to take drugs. He was vicious and raped me when he was in one of his evil moods, and I became terrified of him. It felt like I was his prisoner and, in the end, I thought he was going to kill me. I couldn't escape though. He was so controlling. He always made me think it was my fault; that I'd pushed him until he lost his temper.

'When I first came in here, I had no confidence or self-respect. I felt I was irrelevant, and useless, and that I had no purpose.'

'When did things improve for you?' I asked, taking a sip of my hot coffee.

Chelsea said that her first few days in the classroom were terrifying, but as time wore on, she began to enjoy learning again.

'At first, I felt so stressed. I didn't have good memories of school and it all came flooding back; not being able to understand, feeling like everyone was laughing at me. There was a time when I only cared what the other girls thought about me, and I would mess around to seek their approval and hide my fear through being an idiot.

'I was still doing drugs, but I guess at some point, it changed. A few months in, I realised that I didn't want prison to be the end of me. As I learned more, I began to feel a sense of accomplishment, and the drugs just seemed less important. I had a lot of support and in the end, I started to use my learning as a way of distracting me from thinking about drugs and when I was next going to score. If I concentrated hard enough on my work, I could control the cravings. It was fantastic.

'I found some of the lessons went really fast, and something just "clicked" inside. Once I realised that I could succeed without drugs, it made me feel better about myself and like I could be someone. It's like my brain has woken up and it's a different sort of escape.'

As Chelsea started to change herself, she observed that the people around her had noticed the change in her, and began to seek her advice about how she had found the experience of learning inside.

She told me: 'I say to them: "Take it with both hands because it's something that's for you only; no one can take it away. It will make you feel better about yourself, I promise. Prison may take away so many years of your life, but you can take some of that time back by making use of the time."'

I asked her more about her job in Vita Nova, and what she enjoyed about it.

'The other girls and I have a laugh. It just makes me feel

more normal, like a proper member of society. I'm doing a catering qualification. I want to be able to hold down a proper job when I get out of here and fight to get my daughter back.'

Chelsea told me about other women on her wing who loved their work – one was doing a diploma in counselling, which was part funded by the Prisoners' Education Trust, and she spoke of her friend Sharon, who had done her Level 2 in hair and beauty, after successfully completing her Level 1.

'She left about two months ago, but she always did my nails and hair,' she said. 'Before she left, we worked out a business plan and she's determined to set up on her own and have her own salon. She wrote last week and said her parents are proud of her, and that she's never coming back here.

'She said she no longer feels like she needs to hide her face around town. She's a shining example of what you can do if you focus on the right stuff in here.'

As she said that, the officer announced that the movement freeze had been lifted and they could be escorted back to the house blocks.

'It's been great chatting with you, Chelsea,' I said. 'It's wonderful to learn of a positive outcome from what must initially have been a terrible situation to be in.'

'Yeah, I'd never have thought I could become the person I am now,' she said, and with that we said our goodbyes. As I sipped my coffee and watched Chelsea leave the café,

I thought about another woman, called Nicole, who told me that prison had 'changed her life'.

I met Nicole at a homelessness summit I attended, where we found ourselves sitting next to each other while waiting for our turn to speak. We started chatting and soon realised that we were both as nervous as each other.

She had been asked to speak about her experience of prison and how she coped after she was released. When all the speakers had finished, the delegates were split into small groups to discuss issues surrounding homelessness after release from prison.

Nicole was in my group and was very impressive, and at the end of the day, there was a drinks reception in another part of the building.

I sought her out to continue hearing her story, as I remembered her vaguely from when she first arrived in custody about three years previously, but had never really got to know her very well while she was in prison.

'I am a basic prison statistic,' she told me. She had spent time in and out of care as a child, after being abandoned by her parents. She dropped out of school at 12, was addicted to crack at 13 and heroin at 15. She spent time homeless on the streets of London. During her late teens, she became involved in a relationship with a violent criminal, who was well known to the authorities.

'As the relationship wore on, the crime got worse. It started with him sending me out to shoplift during the day to fund our drug habit, but then when I got back, he would beat me up, saying I was withholding stuff from him. By that point I'd been in a youth offender's place and in and out of Holloway for a few weeks at a time for shoplifting and theft.

'He wasn't only violent towards me, he was also very controlling on different levels; there was a lot of emotional guilt and I had no money. He claimed my benefits, so I had to do what he said.

'He started making me go out with him at night and he was really into knife crime. I would shoplift all day and hang out with him at night; I don't think I ever slept. In the end I was arrested for two knifepoint robberies and handling stolen goods. He was done on about ten counts.

'When I arrived in prison, I had two black eyes and was about six stone. I looked a right mess and felt really ill, but I remember you so well Doctor Brown, 'cos when you saw me in Reception you were the only person who looked me in the eye. Actually looked at me. No one had asked if I was okay until I met you. It's easy to feel invisible and totally worthless when you arrive in prison.'

I was humbled. I didn't remember the encounter, but it was a reminder to me of how important it is to treat people with kindness and dignity. Something so basic had clearly meant so much to her at a time when she was feeling so vulnerable.

We chatted about her recovery. She described being on House Block One as a 'nightmare' and how she was determined to get off drugs while she was in prison. Her sentence was long enough to overcome her addiction and she was desperate to change her life for the better.

She had planned her detox from methadone, and although it was a slow process she stuck to her plan and managed eventually to break free from the hold that drugs had had on her for so many years.

'It felt incredible to finally be free,' she said. 'It's the small things that make the difference. I love having my own mobile phone,' she said, showing me her handset, with a funny screen-saver with a selfie of her in the park. 'And I get to buy the food I want to eat, rather than have what I'm given.'

'It must feel amazing,' I agreed, trying to imagine what it must really feel like to be free after so long behind bars.

For Nicole, her life started to improve in prison when she found work on the cleaning party, where she also gained some recognised cleaning qualifications.

'There were three levels: basic, additional, and specialist, and I got my specialist qualification in bio-hazard cleaning, which basically means cleaning up blood, piss, shit and sick. There's a lot of that in prisons!'

I raised my eyebrows and we both laughed.

'Then after about a year I moved to House Block Four, where I had a cell with my own shower. Doing a good job gave me a sense of achievement. When I first started working, I was so stand-offish, rude and horrible. I didn't talk to anyone. But then I started to make friends with the other women I worked with. I had a sense of self-worth and belonging for the first time.

'People would thank me for working so hard, especially after cleaning up a stinking shitty cell. The worst was after a dirty protest – you know what I'm talking about don't you, Doctor Brown?

I made a face in disgust.

'Yes, I do, it's totally revolting how anyone could behave like that.' Over the years I had encountered many people protesting by smearing their faeces all over the walls and floor in frustration or anger at being in prison or over some other issue they might be having.

'Thought you might! The smell was indescribable. But I coped and I was rewarded for that work.'

Nicole was put on an enhanced regime, which meant she was allowed extra visits, more clothes, additional phone credit and the chance to apply for better jobs.

'I did a lot of courses to try and overcome my mental health issues, and worked with a psychologist to try and get my head straight. I also did a peer mentoring class. My vocational trainer supported me so much and gave me time off to attend the courses; I felt like she was with me every step of the way.'

Nicole described a course around domestic abuse, run by a charity called Aurora New Dawn, as 'completely life-changing'.

'I was in tears a lot of the time, even though I'm not really an emotional person. They made me realise how close I was to death on so many occasions, and how far back my relationship with abuse goes. It completely changed the way I looked at stuff.'

Nicole moved on to Phoenix House and was on ROTL (Release on Temporary Licence) for a few weeks before her eventual release.

Phoenix House opened in April 2019. I was told the name referred to the phoenix rising from the ashes. It is for residents who have progressed on their journey through prison and allows for independent living, and access to employment or to leave the prison on ROTL.

Release on Temporary Licence means the women can leave prison for a certain amount of time each day to work in the community, perhaps with a cleaning or catering company. As well as finding and establishing jobs outside, it can help them reconnect with children and other family members, in preparation for life on the outside. Women with children may gradually spend more time with them. They may start by meeting them for a coffee at The Community Coffee Shop on the outskirts of the prison, followed by another visit to a café or the park in one of the nearby towns for a couple of hours, before building up to an overnight stay at the location they will be released to. This process is put in place in order to help everyone adjust to the changes, including the children, whose lives will undoubtedly have been turned upside down. They may need to get used to having their mother back in their lives again if they have been absent for some time, and it could possibly take as much adjusting to as it might for that person coming back into their lives and starting to parent them again. It must be a tricky path to navigate.

Within Phoenix House there is no curfew and all residents have their own keys, so I imagine that it is a very different experience to being on normal location. Staff aim to remove the hierarchical structure of the normal house blocks, so everyone is responsible for themselves. The women spend a lot of time working on the issues they might face when they get out, including handling difficult emotions, with the aim that once they are 'Through the Gate', they will be able to cope and rebuild their lives. It is a small environment and the women have weekly community groups, to thrash out any issues they may be having with each other in a positive and constructive way.

For Nicole, there was no time to secure work whilst she was on ROTL, but she started getting used to being back outside with a visit to Ashford High Street with her support worker, and then to Staines on the train. Eventually, she was allowed out for the first time on her own. She also talked about how the staff really helped with her interpersonal skills.

'My social skills were pretty rubbish. On the out, I was always in the back of men's cars and in crack houses. I wasn't used to talking normally with people.

'It was a real stepping-stone to being on the outside, and not being on drugs for the first time in years. It felt really strange and quite nerve-wracking at first.'

As we chatted, Nicole's close friend Amy walked over. She had also been invited to talk at the summit. Nicole introduced us and told me that Amy was still on ROTL and living in Phoenix House, and that they had grown close when they lived there together.

Nicole had not long been out of Bronzefield, and she said that she had finally secured a place at supported accommodation in North London.

'It's not been an easy path. Up until my last week in prison I still didn't know if I would have a roof over my head, as nobody seemed to know what was happening.

'It was really scary.'

Amy said, 'I felt for you. In fact, I was really scared and worried about what was going to happen to you'

Nicole explained: 'It was only when one of the managers got everyone together three days before my release date that it got vaguely sorted. I knew if I didn't have a house, I could relapse back onto drugs, and all the progress I'd made would all have been for nothing. I knew I wouldn't be able to survive without drugs if I was homeless and back on the streets. I had no family to turn to, and only had one friend out there. She was the only person that came to visit me in prison, but I knew I couldn't stay with her as she has young kids.

'I'd burnt all my bridges. When I was released, I had to wait until 8 p.m. to be let into a flat where I stayed for a month. It had £400-worth of electric debt, so I had no heating or hot water for a while. It was also in the middle of nowhere, and really remote. I didn't want to furnish it or make it home because I knew I would be moving on.

'I'm now in supported accommodation in an area that

I know well. It's supposed to be for women who aren't using drugs. But it turned out that two of the other girls living there were using, so I told my probation worker in case she thought I might be at it too. That's caused a lot of tension between me and them, because they know it's me who's said something.'

Nicole went on to tell me that she was trying to rebuild relationships with some of her old friends, and that she had secured volunteer work at the local council, supporting service users in areas like mental health and domestic violence.

'I want to be able to give back,' she said.

'How do you cope for money?' I asked her.

'I'm living on Universal Credit, which is tough. I often have to go to food banks for help but, somehow, I manage to get by. It's still early days but I'm determined to turn my life around,' she concluded.

Amy said: 'People's perceptions of prison are narrow-minded, and usually based on nonsense, whether it's about the cells, the food, the staff, the healthcare, the work activities; it's usually negative.

'What people don't hear about enough is the good that prison has to offer. If you do find yourself in custody after making mistakes, it's not the end of the road. If you're willing to make the best out of a bad situation, all the resources are waiting. You just have to want it. Prison gives you a chance to hit the "refresh" button, and gives you the chance to put the past behind you, along with all the negativity and bad habits. Prison allows you to grow, both personally and academically, with the support from the staff and fellow residents. There's something so positive and heart-warming about a group of different women, all at the lowest point in their lives, finding common ground in supporting each other through the highs and lows of the prison regime.'

Nicole nodded: 'When Amy came in, she was a mess, weren't you Ames?' She patted her arm affectionately.

'I'd lost me. I lost who I was and when I arrived at those gates, I didn't even recognise my reflection in the mirror,' Amy explained. 'The last place I expected to find myself was in prison. But here I am, a year later. I put myself back together bit by bit like a jigsaw puzzle, and slowly that dark tunnel that was my sentence had glimmers of light. I moved to Phoenix House and since then I can say, hand on my heart, that I have been the happiest I've been in years, despite the current situation I am in. Being in Phoenix House has changed my life more than I ever thought it could.

'I now work outside the prison on ROTL, using the skills I learnt on the "inside". I am so far from that person who walked into prison twelve months ago. I can see my future and it's bright.'

Nicole said: 'You're doing brilliantly. I can't wait for you to get out too, so we can hang out together.' Their friendship was clearly very strong.

I wished them luck. I had enjoyed chatting with them, as it is so rare to be able to hear of how people progress after they leave prison.

The day drew to a close, so we hugged each other good-bye and wished each other a safe journey home.

I also wished Nicole every success in her determination to stay off drugs and find happiness, and told Amy that I would look out for her at work.

Chapter Eight

'Now I feel like I have a reason to smile'

Kelly was a regular in my Substance Misuse Clinic.

'I am actually straight and have a lovely fella on the outside who is waiting for me but Katie is my lifeline. She's like an angel for me in here.'

I guess whilst it is not something most people probably assume there's much of in prison, from what I have learned over the years there are many people having sex with each other whilst behind bars.

Another way to pass the time and a counterbalance to the loneliness many women suffer inside. Some women I have met have fallen in love and got married and others have entered into a civil partnership whilst in prison.

Unlike in male prisons where homophobia can be rife, if you are a woman in prison, it is very unusual to be singled out or made fun of for a same-sex relationship. Far from it; hooking up with another resident is positively championed. Being 'gay for the stay', or 'getting a bird whilst doing your bird', are just a couple of the phrases that are bandied about. It is fully accepted that some of the women are having sex whilst they are inside. Dental dams and femidoms are available from the sexual health clinic to ensure they are adequately protected from sexually transmitted diseases.

'I've told him all about Katie, but luckily he doesn't seem to care much. I actually think it might even be a bit of a turn on for him. But no one puts labels on stuff in here. It is like a different world.'

Kelly described how awkward her visits were when her boyfriend came to see her, if Katie also had a visit on the same day from her mum or her sister.

'It can feel quite weird sitting there with him and Katie in the same room,' she smiled.

'She's gay on the out and doesn't have a man at home, and wants us to stay together and live together. Be a proper couple. But I'll be out of here in six months and she's got much longer inside, so I'm not sure how that would work out. She's told me that she has changed women before, but I don't think I'm going to be one of them. I love being with her in here, but I can't really see it lasting.'

She added: 'I want to be off methadone before I'm released and stay clean and on the straight and narrow when I get out, and Katie uses, so I'm not sure it would work for that reason as well. I don't ever want to come back to prison, and the only reason I'm here this time is due to drugs, so I'm determined to steer clear of them. Coming to prison has been a real wake-up call.'

Many female prisoners form pseudo families, that are not always sexual in nature but often based on emotional support and protection. Having a social circle and close interpersonal relationships is paramount to contentment and the same values must hold true behind bars.

'She brings me such comfort though and makes me feel far stronger,' she said. 'Without her, I'm not sure I would've got through my time in prison.

'When I first got here, I didn't know what was happening and I was so scared. My head wasn't in a good place. It was only when I got together with her that things started to improve for me. And the sex was just an extra.' She looked coy.

'I had no idea what I was doing the first time and it feels a bit weird knowing that the screws are walking around, but you know, it's just different. You get used to it and accept it for what it is.

'I definitely wasn't looking for love, and I'm not even sure what it is that we have, but I do know that my time feels easier here with her around. She's like my guardian angel.'

Kelly looked up, fiddling with her nails, which she was clearly proud of.

'Wow, they look great Kelly,' I said as I noticed her different coloured nails, which were covered in artistic patterns. They definitely put my short, unvarnished nails to shame.

'Thanks, I had them done yesterday in the salon. My mate Shona did them; she's training for a beauty qualification. They really cheer me up when I look at them.'

'I'm not surprised,' I said.

Kelly continued to tell me about the different relationships in prisons, and how romance can change quickly inside. Each prison is like its own independent ecosystem of people, working and living alongside each other, some women in romantic relationships, some as friends, many indifferent to each other, or even sworn enemies calling each other 'wrong 'uns' at every opportunity.

For many women, other residents can be a source of emotional and practical support when they first arrive in custody. Although as with all friendships, it is sometimes not that straightforward, and whilst many of the prisoners need support, it is not ideal if their new friends expose them to a new set of risks. As in any predominantly female environment, small incidents can turn into huge dramas, as you would expect in a place where many women are being forced to live together in harmony. But the population changes all the time, with lots of new arrivals each day, others being moved on to different prisons, and many being released; nothing stays the same.

Gossip and rumours spread like wildfire and when new people arrive, existing residents often want to know what they are inside for and for how long.

'We do row loads,' she added.

'What about?' I asked.

'Sometimes she says that other girls are looking at me and flirting with me. I can assure you though that I'm not looking at them, that's for sure. We got into a really bad fight once when she accused me of flirting with a new resident.

'It was so bad that we both ended up in Separation and Care for a week.'

I was quite surprised when I heard that. To be put into that separate unit, where prisoners are placed for their own safety or as a punishment, meant the fight must have been serious.

'It was ridiculous how quickly it got out of hand. Things can blow up in seconds in here.

'We're not the worst, though. Some of the women here fight like cat and dog and are constantly being separated.

'The other day my friend Rachel had to be shipped out to another prison 'cos she was always getting into fights with her partner. Their relationship was real love and hate. They didn't seem to know how to just be happy together.' She sighed. 'I really miss Rachel – she was such a laugh. She was a real character. The wing feels totally different without her there.'

'Is that Rachel who was on House Block Three?'

Kelly nodded.

I knew exactly who she was talking about. Some women in prison are unashamed in their moral codes and views of different crimes and their perpetrators, and Rachel was one of these women. When she came to see me about her eczema one day, she proudly told me that she punched another woman so hard after discovering that she was a paedophile, that she had broken her jaw. I had met many paedophiles in my previous job at the high-security men's prison Wormwood Scrubs. Like many others, this is a crime that is most often associated with men, and I am always disturbed when I am reminded that women can commit the same crime.

'When I found out what she done I just went for her, I couldn't control myself.

'I didn't know I had such strength in me. She was a right wrong 'un,' she said. 'She deserved everything she got, the evil bastard. She's a dirty fucking cunting nonce. I'd do it again if I saw her, but she's been moved to another prison. Just as well, as I'd happily kill her if I got my hands on her again after what she done.' Rachel seemed almost possessed with hatred while she recounted her story.

'They say in 'ere that "Snitches get stitches" but nonces get far worse, if I've got anything to do wiv it,' she snarled. 'I ended up down the block on basic for ages and more time added on to my sentence, but I didn't care. It was worth it.'

She came back to the present and smiled.

'I'm a tough old bird, Doctor Brown. If anyone had a go at you, I'd smash them to pieces!' she said.

I smiled nervously. I found it strangely reassuring, but hoped I would never need to call on her for help. It was at such moments that I was reminded of the reality of the strange environment I had chosen to work in.

*

Natasha had come to see me on a Sunday morning with pain in her left leg. She was limping as she walked through the door.

'How long has your leg been hurting?' I asked.

'Since Thursday. I think I've pulled a muscle. I was play-ing football with the officers. It was really fun but it's been really sore since then.'

When I examined her, I couldn't help but notice multiple small circular scars on her legs.

'How did you get these?' I asked, suspecting they were cigarette burns.

Just as she started to tell me her story, a deafening blast cut through the air. The noise was ear-splitting, and for a few moments we sat waiting for the bell to stop. These alarms sometimes left me with a dull headache, but I was so used to hearing it that it was never a surprise.

When the alarm stopped, an officer tapped on the door and poked her head around. 'Freeze on movement, Doctor Brown' she said. I looked at Natasha. 'Tell me about those scars.' She took a deep breath, and began.

'I've been abused all my life,' she said. 'One evil bitch did this to me and took such pleasure in doing it.'

Natasha was in her early thirties and she had been in and out of prison for ten years. She had addiction issues but she was getting on top of them, and her face was rounded and her skin bright.

'I've always known I was gay. When I was 15, I moved in with a woman who I thought loved me. She was twenty years older than me and after growing up in care and never having a mum, it felt like someone was finally looking after me and loving me.

'But she took pleasure in hurting me – it gave her such

a thrill to abuse me. She did this to me,' she said, pointing to the old scars from the cigarette burns on her legs.

'I can't believe how wicked some people are,' I said, with a heavy heart.

When people think of domestic violence, I for one do not think of a woman hitting another woman. I was surprised to learn that there is also a lot of domestic violence within same-sex relationships.

Natasha was controlled and abused by her dominant partner on a daily basis for over five years.

'I didn't know any different, so her behaviour almost seemed normal. It was only when I went to A&E for the third time within a few months, because of the injuries she repeatedly inflicted on me, that I started to question whether she loved me as much as I loved her. Deep down, I knew the answer but didn't want to face up to it.'

As I have seen with many women, the pattern of abuse started as verbal attacks and then escalated into violence.

'She would start arguments about almost nothing; like I was eating my breakfast too loudly. When she hurt me, she would always blame me afterwards and say: "I wouldn't have done that if you hadn't done such and such", or "I was just trying to get your attention so you would talk to me properly."'

Natasha hung her head as she told her story, not looking me in the eye.

'She kept telling me how worthless I was and that if I left her, I would have no one. It got to the point when I just felt like I was treading on eggshells all the time; it was like being on a knife-edge.' Her voice sounded brittle.

'Once I complained to a mate, who just said it was a "catfight". It's true that I sometimes tried to fight back. But for me it always felt like more than a stupid fight. Once she pushed me so hard against the wall that I hit my head really bad, and had such a terrible headache that I just had to spend the rest of the day lying in a dark room.

'We drank a lot and took drugs. I was very depressed, and I'd got to the stage that in the end I really believed I was totally worthless, so I blamed myself for a lot of it.'

'How did you get away from her?' I asked.

'It was when I came back inside for a longer sentence. Before that, she would pick me up from the gate and we'd just follow the same pattern as before.'

Then her face brightened and her eyes sparkled.

'I've never been particularly religious, but I was sharing a cell and my pad mate talked about this group she was part of at the chaplaincy and persuaded me to go with her. She said it helped her feel calm – to quieten the noise in her head. That was when I met Tanisha.'

'Tanisha is your girlfriend now?' I asked.

'Yes, she is. She's amazing. I started going to a prayer group and then to a choir group. There was no real moment when I thought god spoke to me or anything like that.'

At Bronzefield, at least twelve different faiths are represented, including Judaism, Sikhism, Hinduism, Christianity, Islam, Paganism and Buddhism. There are many weekly faith meetings, including worship, prayer classes and studies. If women arrive in prison and their faith is not represented, and they wish to practise their faith whilst in prison, the chaplaincy ensure that suitable provision is organised for them. They regularly have outside speakers and run all sorts of interesting faith-based sessions, and provide the most wonderful support to the women. I am so impressed with the work they do. They are also in charge of the clothes shop called Boo Teek located in Main Street, which receives donations from various very generous people and organisations. The women can buy shoes and clothes, which are priced from a few pence to a few pounds, but they can also be given the items if they have no money. For a woman who comes to prison in July with just the clothes she is standing up in, such as a T-shirt and pair of shorts, a jumper and pair of warm leggings and socks are welcome wardrobe extras on top of regulation prison clothes, especially if she is then released back to homelessness in the depth of winter, as I see happen so often.

'I enjoyed the peacefulness of the place and once I got stable on methadone, it's like the noise in my head stopped and I could think more clearly.'

'How did you meet?' I asked.

'She was part of our prayer group. There was a right mix of us – a professional pickpocket, a couple of "lifers", an old lady who was in for fraud and some others – but it's like we had this special connection. I learnt a lot about forgiveness and kindness. We looked out for each other on the wing.

'We were great friends first and I started to tell her more about my life. I knew I had made some bad choices, especially with my ex, but she made me understand that I was in control of my future. That God would forgive me for my sins. I felt accepted for the first time in my life.'

When so much is stripped away from women in prison, many of them manage to find direction and peace in religious activities.

'I cried for the first time properly in my life during those sessions. The more tears I shed, the more the anger lifted, and I felt better. I was no longer being sent to Separation and Care for bad behaviour, like I was during all my other sentences, and I started to develop better relationships with the officers. But more than that – I fell in love.'

'How long have you been together?' I asked.

'About eighteen months. Tanisha has been out for six months. She comes to see me as much as she can, she writes and I call her every day, and she has set up a proper home for us; it's a small flat in a little block, which has a communal garden and good people living around. For the first time in my life I'm so excited about being on the out. On one hand, I feel quite scared because I'm risking all my emotions, but I also feel safe and so, so happy. I've never felt like this in my life before.

'She has a job as a cleaner, and is hoping that I'll be able to get a job with the same company when I'm released.

'Apparently, the man who owns the company is really friendly and also a Christian.

'And we're going to get married. I can't wait. We thought about applying to get married in here, but I've only got about five months left of my sentence, so not too long to wait. I've finally found someone who'll love me and support me, no matter what. I can't wait for us to do normal stuff together, like cook meals, go to church, and go for walks in the park. Now I feel I have a reason to smile. Everything feels better with her in my life.'

'Congratulations, that's really wonderful' I said, smiling back. 'Planning a wedding can be so exciting.'

'I can't wait to go shopping for our outfits!' she said, with a broad grin.

After checking her leg, I couldn't find any sign of infection or of anything more serious, and told her that she had probably just pulled a muscle as she suspected.

'Would you like to try some Deep Heat or Ibugel?' I asked.

'Yes please, can I have some Deep Heat? I love that stuff,' she replied.

Hearing her story really lifted my spirits and reminded me that sometimes being in prison can have a happy outcome.

*

Being inside for many women is not only hard on them, but also on the people they leave on the outside, their children and partners. Conjugal rights are defined as 'the right of sexual intercourse between man and wife'. These rights are not allowed in any UK prison, though there is some debate about the importance of familial relationships in achieving successful rehabilitation. There are many countries around the world that allow conjugal visits, such as Australia, Canada, Denmark, France, Germany and Spain. In other countries known for their harsh penal systems, like Brazil, Mexico and Russia, conjugal rights are also considered a basic right. Whilst it is traditionally thought of as a chance for sexual contact, campaigners point out that this can cover a range of normal familial interactions. In France, for example, visits last seventy-two hours and take place in small flats with kitchens, dining rooms and other rooms, like a typical home. These visits allow for ordinary familial interactions, such as cooking meals or watching TV together, or for parents to spend time with their children. And in Norway, prisoners are treated as humanely as possible. They have a very progressive and liberal attitude with regular private visits. The official figures show that Norway has by far the lowest reoffending rate in the world, though it is branded 'luxurious' or 'soft' by some.

Release on Temporary Licence is part of the rehabilitation and resettlement of prisoners, and as well as license to go out for training, to help them find work once they are released, or to paid employment, they may be granted a resettlement overnight release licence, to spend a night at the place they will be living once they are released. This is not an easy process and involves a number of risk assessments, internal reports, support from probation and so on, and it is much more about the 'bigger picture' than conjugal rights.

There is debate around whether having sex with your spouse is a basic human right, though in the eyes of the law in this country, prisoners are denied conjugal visits on the grounds that they have no fundamental right to reproduce or have sex. However, it is widely agreed that supportive relationships and regular family contact are crucial to coping in prison and reducing reoffending rates.

For some, however, prison is a place to get away from unhealthy relationships. A very pretty girl came to see me one day in my clinic. As she walked in, I tried to hide my surprise at her appearance.

Claire was young, very slim and no taller than five foot four, but she was hugely out of proportion, due to her very large breast implants. She looked as if she could topple over due to the weight of them.

'Hi, Claire. How can I help you today?' I asked, trying to keep my face neutral.

'It's my tits,' she said, miserably. 'I'm getting pains in the left one, and I'm frightened I might have breast cancer. I know it might sound daft, but it's making me worried that something's really wrong. It's so difficult to check for any lumps and stuff 'cos they're rock hard.' She stretched and rubbed her shoulders absent-mindedly.

'Does your back hurt too?' I asked. She nodded.

'They're so uncomfortable! I don't know if it's the weight

of them, but my back feels constantly achy,' she sighed. 'My sugar daddy wanted me to have them done so he paid for the operation. I had tiny tits before, which I was quite happy with. I really hate them now.

'He called them "silicone perfection" but they feel anything but... ' She did not look proud of them, self-consciously trying to hide her chest with her arms.

'Okay, Claire. Can you pop on to the couch and I'll examine you, if that's all right?'

She was so little that she needed to use the step to get up on the couch.

Once she was lying down, I asked her to take off her top and bra.

'I used to be an A cup, but now I need a double G, so it's quite a difference. I hate it,' she explained.

I even felt uncomfortable for her as she released the fastenings on her bra to let her breasts free, because they were so large and rigid.

With her consent, I gently examined her. In some cases, the implants can move or even burst, but her breasts felt hard and I couldn't feel what was going on under the implants. I had seen a few women with implants as a GP in the community, and remember having to concentrate to appear impartial or unsurprised or judgemental at the size some had chosen for themselves.

When I had finished examining her, she put her bra and oversized T-shirt back on and I asked her some more questions about her surgery and recent symptoms, as well as about any previous problems in her past medical and family history.

'It's so difficult to know exactly what is causing your symptoms,' I said. 'I'm going to refer you to the breast clinic at the local hospital, for a second opinion. If they feel further investigations are needed, they can organise them there and then.'

'That's amazing, thank you. Do you think I'll be able to talk to them about getting these awful implants removed while I'm there?' she asked.

'There's no harm in asking. You won't be able to get it done while you're in prison, I'm afraid, but once you're out, if it's something that you really want to do, then they can advise you. I'm afraid I don't know enough about it – it's not something I see so much of in here.' I smiled apologetically.

'Well, I'm trying to get away from him – my sugar daddy – and as soon as I'm free of him, I want to get them removed. I desperately wish that I'd never gone ahead with it in the first place.'

Claire started to tell me more about herself. Two years before coming to prison, she had been a studying for a nursing degree at a university, some distance away from the market town where she grew up in Norfolk.

'I wanted a more worthwhile career, as I was bored with the office job I'd been in for three years. I've got a young son, and I had to make more money, so I started stripping,' she said, not quite meeting my eye as she spoke.

'I hated doing it, but it was good money. My son was

three and I had no financial support from home,' she explained. 'I would get a sitter two or three times a week, so I could go out and work. One of my new course mates told me she was doing it, and invited me to join her. She said it was the easiest and quickest way to make money. I held down a part-time job at the local coffee shop for a few weeks, but it didn't make sense; I had my fees, rent and Jacob's nursery costs to pay on top of everything else.

'The first time I went to the club, I had no clue what I was doing, but I've always loved dancing. My legs were shaking so much but I got to the end, and got a £100 tip slipped into my underwear,' she said, smiling nervously.

'I met loads of new people, and I loved the social side, but I hated the work and the hours. I used to do some dances and then private lap dances for regulars. When I wasn't on stage I would be walking around the floor, talking to customers, and if they took the bait, I'd take them away to one of the back rooms for a private dance, where I would completely strip off. I could be paid a few hundred pounds at a time for one of them. Sometimes they wouldn't even want me to dance, and I'd just chat to them and listen to them go on and on, like an expensive counsellor. It seemed mad that I could make so much money in such a short space of time.'

'Did you tell anyone about it?' I asked.

'I didn't tell a soul – none of my family or friends – because I was worried that they'd judge me and think badly of me. I was ashamed of what I was doing, if I'm honest,' she replied sheepishly.

'I was never frightened and I loved the money, but I hated the way that some men behaved and would try it on. I also didn't like working so late at night. Sometimes they would linger outside after the club had shut, waiting for us. I hated the drunk men the most as I don't drink. They would always stink of booze and fags, and I would talk to them and have to repeat myself over and over again, but luckily the security staff would move them on, so I never really felt scared. The club looked after us.

'But the hours were long and some nights I didn't get in until 3 or 4 a.m., and then I had to be at lectures at 9. I would always be half asleep, which defeated the object. I started to fall behind with my coursework and was really short-tempered with Jacob. I was just knackered all the time.'

'Is that how you met your partner?' I asked.

'Yeah, Steven came into the club one night. He didn't seem to want anything from me. He was kind, polite, and respectful. We just talked about life and seemed to connect on a deeper level,' she said. 'I was pretty wary – we were in a strip club after all – but I soon started chatting easily with him, and he was so generous. He always tipped me really well.

'He's much older than me, maybe 50 now, but he seemed to genuinely care about me and Jacob, and what I wanted out of life. He ran his own logistics business and had a huge house and three teenage kids. He told me that he and his wife got on but weren't in love any more, and that they led separate lives. I started looking forward to seeing him.'

After coming to the club regularly for a few months, Steven made Claire an offer that she felt was almost impossible to refuse.

'He said he would pay my rent and college fees and our extra costs, plus I would get an allowance from him for clothes and other stuff that I needed. Originally, I wasn't sure what this meant, so I said I would go away and think about it. He just said he wanted to look after me.

'I didn't know at the time that this would make him my sugar daddy, and I'd be what they call a "sugar baby", but I went for it. I guess I was pretty naïve,' she said with an embarrassed shrug. 'I felt like it wouldn't just be about sex, it would be about friendship, and I enjoyed his company.

'And men my own age didn't appeal to me. Me and Jacob's dad parted just after he was born. He was so immature and juvenile, and I had honestly given up hope of finding someone I would enjoy spending time with.'

At first, Claire explained, the arrangement worked. She got on with her studies and saw Steven regularly – about once a week – and he would take her to amazing restaurants and concerts and even sometimes away for the night. He bought her beautiful gifts, like expensive handbags and lingerie. Best of all, a regular cash sum would appear in her account.

'I knew we had an unconventional relationship, but I still thought we had a normal relationship of some description. I thought of him as my boyfriend.'

However, some months in to the relationship, Steven

started to demand more and more from her, and he became more controlling.

'He started by suggesting I change my clothes and my hair. But he never seemed satisfied with what I did,' she explained. 'Then he suggested a boob job, and I reluctantly agreed. I hated the idea of surgery as I was worried about something going wrong but, in the end, Jacob went to spend a few days with his dad's parents, and I had the operation. Steven found the surgeon; I don't know where from. He told me he was good, and I believed him.

'I was in agony when I woke up, but after a few days it wasn't so bad, and he loved them – and could not get enough of them.'

'Is this relationship what led you here? To Bronzefield?' I asked.

She nodded slowly.

'Steven started to tell me that I "owed him". At least once a week he asked me to do some extra work for his logistics firm.'

She rolled her eyes: 'He got me to start carrying packages for him. I knew he worked in logistics, and that he had a lot of money, and I sometimes suspected it wasn't all totally legit. But I didn't feel like I could refuse. Pretty stupid, right? That's why I'm here.

'He also started to push boundaries in bed, and that was where I drew the line.

'One night in bed, he asked me. "Please can you call me daddy? Please call me daddy?" For me, that was a step too far. I mean, did he want me to be his daughter? It made me feel sick.'

It was unusual for patients to offer quite such intimate details about themselves, but I guess it may have helped Claire to make sense of what had happened to her.

'That's when we fell out properly. I refused to have sex for a while. Not long after that, police burst into my flat and seized a bag he'd asked me to look after for him. I swear down I didn't know what was inside, and when I found out it was a stash of class A drugs, I nearly passed out with shock.

'Now we're both locked up, but I'm really hoping to be released on tag in a few months. I can't wait to see my little boy and be his mother again, properly.

'I don't want anything to do with Steven,' she added. 'He wrote to me for a while, begging me to write back and call him, but I've refused, and I think he must have got the message by now. I really hope so anyway.'

'From what you've told me you would be much better off without him, and I'm sure you've got the strength and resolve to find your own way,' I told her. I truly believed it.

'Thanks for listening, Doctor Brown,' she said. 'I feel so much better for offloading on you.'

'You're more than welcome,' I responded. 'I'll do your referral letter today, and hopefully you won't have to wait too long before you get an appointment.'

*

The other topic around sexuality within prisons that I am sometimes asked about is that of trans prisoners. It is something I read about a lot in the papers and again, it is a complex topic. I have met a few trans prisoners over the years, and there is specialist in-house support for these residents within prison. They are well integrated into the community and are given appropriate underwear and toiletries in Reception.

One day during my Sunday morning clinic, I met Melanie.

As she walked in, I noticed she was wearing a wig because it was a bit off-centre. Her eyes were startling because of her heavy bright green eyeshadow, and she wore a colourful patterned dress. It was not in keeping with her black clumpy shoes.

'Hi, Melanie,' I said. 'Take a seat. How can I help you?'

She sat down gingerly, and appeared to be in pain.

'Hello Doctor Brown,' she said, her voice hoarse, as if she'd been a heavy smoker.

'I've been getting really bad belly aches on and off for a while, but it's been much worse since yesterday and I'm really worried about it now.'

'Have you had any weight loss, diarrhoea or vomiting?' I asked.

'I vomited last night,' Melanie replied, and went on to tell me more about the pain that was now constant and much worse in her lower abdomen.

'Do you mind popping on to the couch so that I can examine you?'

She slowly stood up and eased herself up on to the couch, obviously in a lot of pain. When I started to examine her, she looked a little anxious.

'I'm still waiting to have my surgery,' she volunteered, possibly preparing me to not be surprised with what I was about to find.

'I have been on the waiting list for gender reassignment for ages and I'm beginning to give up hope of it ever happening,' she said looking miserable and lost in her thoughts.

I gently examined her and found that she was extremely tender in her lower abdomen, but there was no swelling in her groin or scrotum.

'I think you have appendicitis,' I explained, 'so I'll arrange for you to go hospital and get it sorted out.'

Melanie looked relieved, which surprised me a little.

'Oh, that's such a relief," she said, 'I was convinced I had bowel cancer. Trouble is in prison, there's too much time to dwell on things and your mind plays tricks on you and blows everything out of proportion.'

'I bet it does, it must be awful,' I said, trying to imagine how hard it must be to control intrusive thoughts and fears when you have too much time on your hands.

'Get yourself back to the house block now Melanie and I will sort everything out for you,' I reassured her. She thanked me and slowly walked away.

That was the first and last time I ever saw Melanie, and I heard that soon after returning from hospital following an appendicectomy, she was transferred to another prison.

Upon entry into prison, prisoners must provide a Gender Recognition Certificate showing they are already being treated for gender dysphoria. If they have this certificate, prisons are legally required to move them to a prison of their gender.

If prisoners do not have a certificate, transgender prisoners will have to be referred to the Gender Identity Clinic (GIC) by the prison doctor or psychiatrist, and will need to live the role for two years before starting hormones and receiving an official diagnosis.

There is an argument that without these precautions prisoners could simply be making a 'lifestyle choice', thinking a female prison might be an easier environment to survive in than a male prison.

Melanie reminded me a little of another trans prisoner, Judy, who I met not long after starting to work at Bronzefield. She was very chatty, and I remember her telling me how much she had hated being in Pentonville prior to transferring to Bronzefield.

'It was real shit there,' she had said. 'People had no understanding of what it feels like to be in the wrong body. It's not a choice, it's who I am.'

*

There are now a significant number of transgender women in female prisons, but some are being moved back to male prisons after a prisoner by the name of Karen White sexually assaulted two women whilst on remand at New Hall jail in Wakefield, and also admitted to raping two women before being sent to prison. The story was in the national press and the prisoner, who was born male and identifies as female, was described as a 'predator' to women and children by a judge. It is clear that it can be hard to balance the needs of transgender prisoners against those of the prison population, and this is perhaps the crux of the issue.

The UK's first prison unit for transgender women opened at HMP Downview, a women's prison in Surrey, in 2019, initially housing three prisoners with gender recognition certificates.

This is such a highly sensitive issue, but I have to admit that I worry for the mental wellbeing of some of the vulnerable, fragile and damaged women in prison, being in the company of someone who may have committed violent offences against women. My encounter made me realise that for those people who are genuinely isolated and suffering from this condition, where there is distress because of a mismatch between their biological sex and their gender identity, prison must be an incredibly tough place to end up.

Chapter Nine

**'I had to reach rock bottom before
I could pull myself back up'**

It was a freezing cold Sunday morning in December with a biting wind that felt as if it was getting into my bones. I pulled my coat tight around me and walked across the bleak, depressing tarmac yard towards the main part of the prison, otherwise known as Main Street. The high walls and barbed wire surrounds did nothing to cheer the scene up. After unlocking and locking again the solid metal door and then the gated door, the warmth of the prison was strangely comforting, as was the smell of breakfast wafting down from the cafeteria upstairs.

A group of girls passed me on their way to work in the kitchen, accompanied by an officer. They all smiled at me and a couple of them said, 'Hi, Doctor Brown.' And a strange sense of belonging washed over me.

As usual, I had no idea who I would be seeing in my clinic that day, and there was always that same familiar sense of apprehension as to what the day would bring and what I would be confronted with.

What stories I would hear. What dramas would unfold.

As I was unlocking the gates to Healthcare, the officer in charge of the prison that day greeted me with a smile.

'Hi, Doc,' he said.

'Morning,' I replied. 'How are you?'

'Busy. I hope you won't need to send any out to hospital today. Three went out yesterday, so we're really short-staffed with three bed watches,' he warned me. 'It's not been easy.'

Whenever a prisoner is sent out to hospital, they are always accompanied by two or more officers, depending on the level of risk, and if they stay in hospital they remain on a 'bed watch', which means constant supervision by prison staff. This can spread staff quite thinly and make running the prison even harder.

'I'll try not to,' I assured him as I hurried past. But I knew that if I thought anyone needed to go to hospital, I would have to send them, no matter how many bed watches there were.

A warming smell of toast and coffee hit me as I walked along the corridor to my small windowless room. I logged on to the computer, anxious to see what was in store for me. The list was full, as was the list for repeat prescriptions. Some names were new to me, but there were many familiar names as well.

By 10 a.m. I had finished most of the rescripts and I could hear the waiting room fill with noise.

The door opened.

'Morning Doctor Brown!' Susan, the Healthcare Assistant, came in with a cheery grin.

'I think we are in for some drama today,' she said, as she pulled up a chair at the tiny desk opposite mine. 'Ellie is back in again.'

I groaned. Ellie was in her early forties and from a very troubled background. She was in and out of prison every few months, or sometimes even weeks, and was notoriously difficult for prison staff to deal with. She had an extensive and imaginative history of self-harm, which usually involved inserting anything possible into any orifice on offer. The last time I saw her, she had rammed an unfolded paper clip into her ear and perforated her eardrum. Whenever any of us saw Ellie's name on our lists, we would roll our eyes. We knew her stay was unlikely to be without incident, and that she would almost certainly end up having a trip or two to the local hospital.

'What's she done this time?'

'She's shoved her asthma inhaler up her arse,' Susan said. I sighed, exasperated before I had even started the clinic. 'She says she's bleeding and in pain.'

However many times I encountered self-harm, the horror it struck in me never diminished.

There are many prisoners with personality disorders, who also suffer from other complex mental health issues. These prisoners can demonstrate particularly challenging and difficult behaviour, including self-harm. Managing them in the prison system can be exceedingly difficult.

Ellie would often self-harm at the weekend because she knew that she was likely to be sent out to hospital, escorted by officers, and that this would cause short-staffing within the prison. She also very often made allegations against staff, and so all encounters had to be recorded on body-cam – a camera worn by prison officers on top of their clothes. Ellie's explanation for self-harming was that voices in her head were controlling her and telling her she was evil and needed to harm herself. To most people it would appear to be attention seeking, but the underlying psychiatric picture was much more complex.

The first lady to be seen I knew well. She was a large lady in her early sixties called Caroline, who had been in prison for many years. As I brought her notes up, my computer froze. This often happened when a prisoner's notes were extensive.

I cursed under my breath – I only had ten minutes for each appointment and if I started running late this would only get worse as the day went on. I took a deep breath, sipped my coffee and waited for the computer to catch up.

Caroline had awful issues with self-harm, and this was part of the reason for her long notes. The last time I had seen her, she was complaining of abdominal pain and she'd told me that over the previous six months she had swallowed a variety of objects including a plastic knife, fork, spoon, three pens and some paper clips.

When I examined her, I found that her abdomen was tender and distended. She had to be admitted to hospital and had remained there for ten days. I was worried that she was on the list to be seen today because she may have been swallowing some more bits and pieces.

'Caroline, how are you feeling? Are you having stomach pains again?'

She shook her head. 'Don't worry, Doc, not this time. I've just got a really itchy rash on my feet. It's driving me crazy.'

What a relief, I thought as I checked her feet. It was clear she was suffering from athlete's foot and I told her I would prescribe some anti-fungal cream.

I couldn't help but ask. 'So, what happened last time you went to hospital?'

'They took me to theatre for surgery,' Caroline announced. 'They found all the things I had swallowed, but the knife had perforated my bowel.' She paused for a moment and looked deep into my eyes. 'Thank you for sending me to hospital, Doctor Brown. I feel much better now.'

'I'm not surprised, Caroline,' I replied. 'I hope it's put you off swallowing any more things.' I smiled and, to my joy, she smiled back, which was a rare sight on her usually expressionless face. There is always something heart-warming about sharing even a small smile or a little laughter with the women, especially a sad and damaged soul like Caroline.

Just as Caroline left, the alarm sounded again and there was a freeze – nobody would be allowed to move around the prison until it was lifted. Sometimes the freeze on movement is a total pain but some days if I am running a bit behind it can be a welcome relief.

As I am only allocated ten minutes for each patient, if everyone turns up late, it can be a very unpleasant way to work. Moreover, many of the women I see have complex issues to deal with, so I very rarely manage to complete the consultation in the ten minutes anyway. I find it almost impossible.

While the freeze was in place, I spent the time finishing off Caroline's notes, typing up the consultation in full, checking pathology results to look for any abnormalities that might need actioning, and checked the rescript list to see if anymore prescription requests had been added by the nurses.

After about twenty minutes, I heard loud shouts and screaming coming from the waiting room at the end of the corridor. Was movement back on? I stuck my head around the door, only to catch Susan's eye as she hurried down the corridor. She shook her head.

'No movement yet,' she said, with a frustrated expression. 'Punch-up in the waiting room.'

It turned out that two of the women who were waiting to go back to their house blocks knew each other on the outside. They hated each other, and were deliberately kept on different wings in the prison. But they couldn't hold back when they were face-to-face in the waiting room.

'It took three of us to pull them off each other,' Susan said.

'One had grabbed a clump of the other's hair. I've just chucked a handful of it in the bin. It was brutal.'

Eventually the freeze was lifted and so I could carry on with the clinic. Susan went off to bring the next patient in, and came back with Ellie.

'Hi, Ellie. How are you today? Are you back for long?' I asked, trying to be bright and breezy, dreading hearing about what she may have done to herself.

'Hi Doctor Brown. No, only two weeks this time. Came back two days ago. I told the nurse I'd stuck my asthma pump up my arse, but I haven't. I made it up 'cos I was bored. I feel fine and don't really need to see you today.'

'What a relief! Thank Heaven you haven't harmed yourself again. You've just made my day, Ellie,' I said and we both smiled. While my time is in short supply and I usually hate it when people waste it, there is an element of pastoral care to my role and it was good to hear that she was in good health and good spirits. It was the first time that I had ever seen her when she hadn't self-harmed.

'Try and be good while you're here. Don't let the voices get the better of you if possible,' I said.

'Yeah, I'm getting better at not letting them control me as much, which feels brilliant. Thanks, Doctor Brown.' And with that she stood up and Susan escorted her back to the waiting room.

For the first time since meeting Ellie I was left with a positive, maybe naive, feeling of hope that maybe her life was going to get better after all.

*

The next name on my list was new to me. Diane was in her late forties and had never been in prison before.

As she walked in, I was surprised by her clipped tones and immaculate nails. Her brown hair was in a perfect bob and her jeans and shirt were obviously expensive.

'Hi, Diane, I'm Doctor Brown. What can I do for you today?' I asked.

'I've come about my anti-depressants,' Diane said. 'I'm starting to feel much better but the GP I saw a few weeks ago told me to come back after I'd been on them for about a month to check whether I'm on the right dose, as he told me that it could take a few weeks before I would know if they're helping or not.'

'Oh, okay. Have you ever been on anti-depressants in the past?' I asked her.

'No, but they really seem to be helping,' she told me. 'I feel much brighter and less hopeless.' She beamed a warm smile with perfectly straight teeth.

'How long have you been here for?' I asked her.

'This is my sixth week,' she replied. 'I'll be out on tag in a couple of months, I hope. I'm here for shoplifting and fraud.'

As we started talking, Diane told me more about what had led to her being in prison.

She appeared to come from a wealthy background, and went on to tell me that she lived in West London in a beautiful family home. As she talked it seemed that she had a gilded lifestyle and did not want for anything.

But Diane had a problem with alcohol that had changed everything for her.

'For the first ten years of my marriage, life was great,' she told me. 'We travelled abroad a lot and I never needed to or wanted to work. I enjoyed myself and always found things to fill my time.'

'That sounds wonderful,' I said.

'It was, but then things changed. My husband James was made redundant from his job in the city and I started to drink too much.'

She exhaled sadly.

'I was drinking far too much and was also really bored,' she said. 'We were forced to economise, and I started to drink more and more.

'Then one day, I walked into a shop and took a handbag from the stand. It was a middle-of-the-range-one, I think, but I liked the colour. I simply put it over my shoulder, strolled around the display and walked out of the shop. It was so easy and gave me a real buzz.'

She looked embarrassed, remembering the rush of energy and the feelings that shoplifting gave her.

'Then a few weeks later, I saw a stunning dress in a local boutique. I'd been a regular customer there and knew the staff well. I went to try it on in the changing rooms and saw it didn't have a security tag, so the alarm would not go off when I went out. I knew it must've been a return. I put it in my bag without really thinking about what I was doing. I was on such a high as I walked down the street, away from the shop.'

I was surprised by how open she was being about her behaviour, but kept my face impassive.

'I could actually afford the items I took, but I did it for the thrill of it. Then I started to shoplift every week. That, and I went to lunch with friends and to the gym, of course. My weakness was always shoes, handbags and clothes. It became a compulsion. Big department stores, small designer boutiques, gift shops; I stole from them all.'

'Were you ever caught?' I asked.

She sighed.

'Yes, on a couple of occasions, but I talked my way out of it. When you sound like I do, it wasn't too hard to convince the police with whatever excuse I could think of,' she continued. 'I often said that it was all a mistake and I had simply forgotten to pay. No one expected me to be taking things. I'd start crying, and they would end up comforting me. I got away with it. I am so ashamed of myself when I think back.'

She shrugged her shoulders.

After her husband's redundancy, he found another job. Six months later, he asked Diane for a divorce, saying he had met someone else at work, and he no longer loved her or wanted to stay married.

'Apparently, it was the girl in the accounts department,' she explained. 'They had been seeing each other for months behind my back, sneaking about at work, and all those trips away were apparently nights at hotels. What a cliché. What's worse was I didn't have a clue. I tried to suggest counselling, but he wasn't interested.'

'Did that make your problem worse?' I asked gently.

'Yes, it hit me so hard. And with less money I felt compelled to steal more.

'I often took stuff after I'd been drinking at lunch,' she said. 'I don't know why I did it. Every time I took something, I thought, *This will be the last time,* but it never was. I didn't think I was harming anyone, and I always felt this high and then a rush of calm afterwards. It was just something that happened. I had to have my designer fix. It was always just the extras and it made me feel good.'

I nodded. Like many shoplifters, Diane's feelings of relief at getting away with it would be tempered by guilt and remorse.

'Sometimes, when I looked at the items, it made me feel a bit sick, so I sometimes gave them away,' she said. 'One time I even tried to sneak something back into the shop. And most of the time I was half-cut. Not that that's an excuse, but I was never thinking clearly about what I was doing. I knew I needed help as it was so compulsive, but I felt so ashamed, I couldn't admit my problem to anyone.'

There is a clinical definition for the urge to steal: kleptomania, and many kleptomaniacs steal without forethought, and their experience of shoplifting has nothing to do with money. Soon, Diane's habit caught up with her.

'I started to run out of excuses and the tears didn't work after a while. The police gave me a caution, but I never thought I would end up somewhere like this.'

'What happened?'

'After the divorce went through, I wanted to keep the house. We still had a big mortgage, so I got a part-time job with a wealthy local businessman who owned a property development company. Then I started to steal from him – mostly cash, and a few forged invoices.

'It was easy,' she said. 'I was in charge of the office and the cash. I was drinking so much by that point – it just freed me from feelings of guilt, worry and fear. Some days I would take vodka in my handbag for an 11 o'clock break.'

'Have you always struggled with alcohol?' I asked.

'I was such a quiet and shy kid,' she told me. 'My first drink at 15 took away the crippling shyness and self-consciousness. I had a new and happy feeling inside, and I found it easy to talk to people and dance at parties. Before that, I was always on the sidelines. Never the person in the middle of the action; my parents even used to call me "mouse". From that day on, any teenage pursuits that didn't involve drinking, I was no longer interested in.

'I drunk my way through university and half the time I would pass out wherever the party was, and would dread the mornings when I would have no idea of what happened the night before. I never intended to get into such a state.

'Then I met my ex, James, and life got so much better. I still drank too much, often on my own and at home, but we would also drink together and a glass of wine at 7 o'clock was just what we did. We also often went to expensive restaurants and would manage to drink a bottle of expensive wine each.

'But weeks would go by when I didn't drink, and I definitely didn't drink in the morning back then, but the truth is that as soon as I had a drink, nothing could stop me. The brakes never went on.'

This was a story I had also heard many times: tales of people who just can't, or don't even know that they should, stop their drinking.

'In my early forties, I tried to control my drinking, but ended up spending most of my days in a torment of sweaty and shaky anxiety. I felt like I couldn't quite function or control my limbs properly. It's hard to explain.

'I always managed to look smart and presentable though, and I made a point of being polished, but I dreaded the nights without alcohol to send me to sleep. I would lie awake, quivering, my mind racing. I did try to stop, and sometimes I managed for a while but could never properly see it through.

'Then when the divorce started, I drank my way through all the emotions. In the end, I would pour a glass of wine before I even opened those brown envelopes.'

Alcoholism is not an exciting disease. Sometimes, it does not involve abusiveness or violence; it is a slow suffering. As with drugs, alcohol feeds a natural selfishness and it thrives on secrecy. It is often associated with pubs, bars and going out, but for some, it is the opposite to this. Often, the more a person becomes addicted to alcohol, the more they try to hide it.

'My friends would frequently have a bottle of wine at

lunch or dinner, but I would drink tonic water or orange juice when I was with them,' she told me. 'Saying I was doing dry January or "taking a break" from alcohol. I would leave the restaurant and go home early to open a bottle of wine and get drunk on my own. I'm not sure how I reached that point.

'I would wake up feeling awful every day. I had stomach cramps and had a continuous headache, but by 11 o'clock I would be planning my next drink. It was a horrible, vicious cycle. The crazy thing is I didn't look like or consider myself an alcoholic. I had a degree, a beautiful home, and a great life; I just didn't fit the bill.'

I nodded. 'And what finally happened to bring you to prison?'

'I already had a caution and a series of fines for shoplifting, but I was arrested for fraud when my boss noticed some money was missing and I ended up here.'

'How are you coping with being in prison?'

'Honestly, when I was finally caught, it was almost a relief. But when I was sentenced, I was terrified. I had no idea what I was going to do. I felt quite desperate. But it's not been as bad as I was dreading. I mostly keep myself to myself, and fortunately I managed to get a job in the garden, which I love. I've also been reading lots of books, which I've borrowed from the library, and that has kept me busy to an extent. I haven't managed to concentrate on a book for years and had forgotten how much I love reading. It's such a wonderful escape from reality.'

'It is. I enjoy reading, too. Have you managed to keep busy in other ways?' I asked.

'I'm a member of the Bronzefield Bees WI and a few other groups,' she said. 'Last week we held a coffee morning and craft fair, which was very enjoyable. I've learnt some new skills and also got to know some wonderful people from all sorts of different backgrounds, and everyone is very supportive of each other. It's groups like that that help to keep life normal in here. Well, as normal as it can be.'

'Do you have any family on the outside?' I asked.

'Not really,' she replied. 'James has got a new girlfriend and doesn't want to know. She's only 35 and apparently they're having a baby. Only one of my friends writes to me now; her husband and James play golf together. She thought I would want to know.'

She looked thoughtful and her eyes were glassy with tears.

'We never had kids. We tried to have a family for a while, but it didn't work out, and he said he wasn't bothered, and at the time, I didn't think I was either. We had such a great lifestyle and went out so much. A baby didn't seem to fit in with that, so we never investigated why I never fell pregnant. Looking back, maybe it would've been the best thing that could've happened for us,' she said looking thoughtful.

'Sometimes it's just not meant to be,' I said, not knowing quite what else to say.

She continued: 'The house has been sold, so I imagine I'll need to rent a flat when I'm released. I can't imagine

I can return to where I lived; gossip spreads like wildfire around there and everyone will know what's happened. I will definitely be persona non grata – no more charity-lunch invitations for me.'

Diane sighed. It was like she had drawn a line under her previous life.

'My sister lives in Bristol, so I might try to find a flat to rent near there, and hopefully spend time with her. We grew apart when I was in London. She's married to a builder, so we led quite different lives. It would be good to get to know my two nieces better. I was never really interested in them when they were small; definitely not the aunty that you might expect. They always seemed to be whining and shrieking. They're teenagers now, so hopefully I can be their friend. I'm looking forward to a fresh start. I'll also need to find a job, of course. I'm not sure what I'll do and now, with a criminal record, it will be even harder.'

When I was a GP in the community, I used to see many people who were damaged by alcohol. It can have a variety of detrimental effects on the body, including liver damage, high blood pressure, damage to the heart muscle, and brain cells, and can also affect mood and mental capacity.

One of the most horrific cases I saw was a woman in her early forties who had been a heavy drinker for years. One day her husband called for an urgent home visit as he said that she had vomited blood, but little did I know how much blood until I got there.

When I got to the house, I found her collapsed on the

floor. Blood was splattered everywhere; across the carpet, all over the sofa, and even up the walls. It looked as if a blood bomb had exploded. I shouted at her husband to call 999 immediately. I suspected she had most likely suffered from ruptured oesophageal varices, distended veins at the base of the oesophagus usually caused by alcohol damage to the liver; a potentially life-threatening condition.

To my massive relief the ambulance soon arrived. The paramedics inserted a line for IV fluids, and within minutes she was on her way to hospital. But it wasn't enough to undo the years of damage to her body that the alcohol had done, and tragically she did not survive the journey.

I was surprised to see that despite her years of alcohol abuse, Diane did not have lasting physical health issues. She had some blood tests done shortly after arriving in prison and when I checked them, to my amazement, I could see her liver function was normal.

'I still think about alcohol; of course, I do,' she told me. 'Some days I think of it even more fondly than my ex, but I am determined to stay sober and will continue with AA meetings when I get out. I'll never go back to drinking. I don't want to feel ashamed any more.'

'It sounds like you're doing really well, and it's wonderful that you're feeling so much better,' I said.

'Yes. So much better,' she explained. 'I can actually sleep now – despite the noise in this place! The shouting and banging never ends but once I drift off, that's it. When

I wake up in the morning, I actually feel rested and can remember what happened the night before!

'Even though I'm waking up in prison I don't feel that awful fear and dread that I used to when I was drinking. It might sound silly, but I almost look forward to the day now, and can remember things in a way that seemed impossible before. Also, I no longer feel exhausted all the time.'

I smiled as she concluded her story, and we agreed that there was no need to change the dose of her anti-depressants for the time being, but I arranged to see her again before her release just to check that she was still okay.

As I left that Sunday, I thought of Diane, and hoped that life wouldn't be too difficult for her when she was released. I see many women with such desperate stories, but there are also those like Diane whose lives have simply slipped off the tracks. One well-spoken lady I remember seeing during one of my Reception shifts had been driving home from an after-work drink to celebrate a colleague's promotion. As she was steering her car down the pitch black country roads, she hit a young man who was crossing the road. He sustained life-changing injuries and she ended up in prison. When I met her the day she arrived in custody, she was in shock and denial, as well as overwhelmed with guilt. 'I just didn't see him,' she repeated over again. Another woman I met had murdered someone when she was drunk. She told me that she had absolutely no recollection of doing it and struggled desperately to come to terms with her reality and her guilt. Neither woman could get their head around the nightmare they found themselves in.

Over the past decade, there has been a lot of debate within the medical world about the classification of alcohol. Some claim that it is more harmful than class A drugs like heroin or crack, because of the damage it can do not only to individuals, causing illness and injury, but within communities too, as a result of the relationship breakdowns and unemployment that it can lead to.

Many more people in the UK are physically dependent on alcohol than on drugs, but far fewer see it as a problem. As it is generally socially acceptable, many people manage to function despite their addiction. It is normalised, so it can be hard to spot those who have a problem.

*

The following week, I arrived for my Sunday-morning shift. It was early, just before 8 a.m. As I walked towards the sliding doors of the staff entrance to get into the airlock, I was joined by an elegant, striking-looking woman in her fifties with beautiful long dark hair, who I had never met before.

There was no one else around and so we started chatting.

'Morning,' I said, as I smiled at her.

She was not wearing a prison belt and key pouch, so I thought she was most likely a visitor, but it was unusual to see anyone early on a Sunday that was not a member of staff, other than possibly a visiting chaplain.

'Good morning,' she replied. 'It's icy cold this morning, isn't it? Do you work here or are you just visiting like me?'

'I'm just one of the doctors,' I explained. 'I work most Sundays and have done for the past four years nearly. I didn't think I would last but somehow I'm still here!'

The door slid slowly open to let us into the airlock, slid shut, and then the second door opened to let us in. We both then pressed our fingers on the biometric, and the next barrier opened to let us through in turn.

'Oh, it must be a fascinating place to work,' she said as she waited to be handed a visitor's badge by the officer. 'I've been invited here by the chaplaincy to give a talk to the residents about how they can turn their lives around.'

As she said that, the officer told her that he had let the duty chaplain know she was waiting to be collected.

'That sounds interesting. What are you going to talk about exactly?' I asked.

The lady introduced herself as Rani. 'I am a recovered alcoholic,' she said. 'I've been sober for fourteen years. I like to tell other people my story in the hope that they'll feel inspired to change their lives, too. I've visited quite a few prisons now, but never a women's prison. I think it will feel quite strange and I must admit I feel a little nervous.'

'Don't be. I am sure the women here will feel really inspired by your story,' I told her.

'In my talks I don't hold back,' she smiled. 'I tell them exactly how it was and how bad things got for me.'

'You sound like you've got a story to tell,' I smiled.

'I started drinking young, and was popular at school as "the life and soul of the party",' she told me. 'I could always out-drink anyone who I was with. I never wanted the party to end. My drinking continued through university and then into my first job as a management consultant.

'At that time, my drinking was under control. I worked hard and played hard but always had the stamina I needed. I went on to get married and we had a beautiful home and three amazing children. My husband liked to drink but not as much as me, and eventually we started arguing about how much I drank.

'When the kids were small, I started to drink more and more. I'd lost my own mum and was feeling overwhelmed with grief, and there was a deep gnawing emptiness inside of me.'

'That sounds tough,' I replied.

'God it was. It was an awful time. When they were all at school, I would drink every night after getting home from work. I would do it to "take the edge off the stress of the day" and I started having blackouts. I never took responsibility for my drinking; I would always blame someone else. It was never my fault, always someone else's.'

She rolled her eyes and brushed a few stray dark hairs from her face.

'Coming from the Asian community only made me feel more ashamed and in denial. My parents' generation could be quite judgemental, and I didn't feel as if I could talk to anyone about it. I was close to my aunties, but I didn't dare speak up about it. I would wake up feeling so awful that the only thing that would make me feel better was more alcohol. I was so jittery. Some days I would promise myself I wouldn't drink that day, but by 6 p.m. I'd have a glass of wine in my hand. Some days I would have a drink before I even got to my desk. There was a shop nearby that sold alcohol, and I would put an appointment in my diary every day, so I could leave my desk and go to buy some.'

Soon, Rani could no longer function at work and do her job properly. She was losing weight quickly and she had awful lower back pain.

'I was asked to leave, and felt relieved. By then, I had intense cravings all the time. I needed my daily fix of alcohol every few hours. I would just sit by the window drinking. My husband and I divorced, and he stayed in the house with the kids.'

The façade she had kept swiftly faded as her life unravelled and her health began to deteriorate.

She said: 'My husband was fed up of dealing with me, and I don't really blame him. I would get emotional and scream and shout at him when I was drunk. My friends all drifted away. In the end, I became suicidal; I could see no point in carrying on. I had reached rock bottom and ended up living in a shed at the bottom of the garden. I was out of control.'

'How hard that must've been,' I replied. I could tell from the way she was speaking how Rani must've reached a very low point. 'How did you manage to turn things around?'

'It was one of the doctors. One day he told me that if I didn't stop drinking, it was going to kill me. In my heart, I knew he was right and when I was actually confronted by it, the thought of dying terrified me.'

I could see the fear in her face as she remembered how frightened she had been, realising what could happen if she continued to drink.

'I realised that I didn't want to kill myself. I wanted to live.'

She took a deep breath, her voice hard.

'Until being told that, I had taken life for granted. It's only when I faced losing it that I realised how precious it is. It all became clear and it was only then that I knew I had to do something to save myself. I couldn't have sunk any lower. I now know that I had to reach rock bottom before I could pull myself back up. I knew that I could either end my life or turn it around. It is hard, really, to put it into words, but I just knew something incredibly powerful was reaching out to me. I'm not particularly religious, but an overwhelming sense of love seemed to engulf me at that moment.'

As she said that I could feel goose bumps on my arms.

'I wanted to live a life free of alcohol, and I knew I wasn't the only one. I no longer wanted to black out every night and be my family's dirty secret. I finally accepted that I needed help. I called a helpline and borrowed some money from my sister to go into a private rehab clinic, and then joined a twelve-step fellowship that helped me stay sober.

'For the first time, I came out of isolation and could finally address my problems and talk about my addiction.

I started the long hard road to recovery and believe me, it hasn't been easy. But I feel extremely lucky.'

Rani came across as incredibly confident and self-assured, and had obviously made a big success of her life. She told me she had since trained as a counsellor and spent a lot of her free time travelling around a number of prisons and young offender institutions to talk to people from all different walks of life to give them hope.

'I know many people find it difficult to admit that they have a problem,' she said. 'But I want people to realise that they can change their lives and find themselves again. They can come back from the void.

'I want to inspire other people. The longer people wait to get help, the worse it gets. But they can start all over again. I've done it, so I reckon anyone can. Sobriety has changed my life; I have a peace now that I never knew possible.'

Rani summed her mission up perfectly: 'We live in a culture that to some extent celebrates drinking, but the reality is, there are much better things than the bottom of a glass. It feels amazing to finally be present.'

Just as she was finishing her story the chaplain arrived to escort her off to meet the women. We said our goodbyes as I went to get my keys from the cabinet and head off to work.

I felt hugely inspired by her, and I hoped that whoever was lucky enough to meet her that day and listen to her story would be too. Maybe they might be able to envisage a brighter future.

Chapter Ten

'When you become hopeless your behaviour becomes increasingly erratic'

I was just finishing entering my notes on the computer at the end of quite a gruelling day in the Substance Misuse Clinic on House Block One when someone tapped gently on the door.

I paused.

This was unusual; normally any knocks on my door were loud and demanding. They could sometimes feel quite threatening and intimidating.

I knew I shouldn't open it. I felt emotionally wrung out and ready to go home after a long day, and was looking forward to relaxing and catching up on the TV drama I had been watching.

Despite my reluctance, I stood up and opened it.

Standing in front of me was a petite young lady in her mid-thirties with very short, brown cropped hair and a tiny butterfly tattoo on the side of her neck. She had a sense of urgency and desperation about her. Her wide green eyes were immediately engaging.

'I'm so sorry to bother you. I know I don't have an appointment but the IMB lady said you would listen to me and help me.'

IMB stands for the Independent Monitoring Board and consists of independent and unpaid members of the public, who ensure that proper standards of care and decency are maintained in prisons. Members have unrestricted access to every part of the prison and can talk to any resident if they wish to. They also have access to prison records, but not to any resident's medical records. They visit regularly on a rota system and play an important role in dealing with issues in prison that may not be dealt with via the normal channels. Residents can make requests to see members about any issue, including worries over visits, lost property, or even more serious concerns, such as bullying. Their role is really valued by the residents.

'Please, please let me talk to you,' she urged, her eyes darting around my room and her feet moving constantly.

'I really need my meds sorted properly,' she pleaded. 'I feel awful.'

'Okay, let me have a look through your records,' I replied. 'Have a seat.' I hadn't the heart to send her away; she looked so anxious and desperate.

Her medication had been wrongly prescribed since her recent transfer from another prison, and it took ages to go through her extensive notes to ascertain the reason why she had been prescribed pregabalin. The rules surrounding pregabalin prescribing are extremely strict in prisons because of issues with addiction, trading and abuse. The only way any resident in Bronzefield can be maintained on a constant dose of pregabalin is if it has been prescribed by a consultant within the previous six months. In Kim's case, it had been prescribed by a consultant psychiatrist with the advice that she should remain on the same dose due to her extreme and severe generalised anxiety disorder, which was due in part to the impact of her IPP sentence.

Once I had found that precious and vital entry in her notes, I knew I could put her back on the dose she needed to keep her stable, as opposed to the detox regime she had been prescribed, without the fear of another doctor decreasing it again prior to her next psychiatric review.

'Your notes go back years, Kim,' I said. 'How long have you been in prison?'

'I got an IPP sentence in 2007,' she told me. 'And I'm still here… ten years later.'

'Wow, that's crazy. How much longer will you be in prison for?' I asked. 'What happened?'

'I just nicked a handbag.'

I was astonished. 'Why are you still here?'

To my embarrassment, despite all the years I had worked in prisons, I had never really understood the significance, or even the meaning for that matter, of an IPP sentence until I met Kim.

Imprisonment for Public Protection sentences were introduced in 2005 and enabled judges to set a minimum term, but no maximum term, to be served. In Kim's case, the minimum term was set at two and a half years, minus the time spent on remand; this expired almost a decade before I met her. After any minimum term has passed, prisoners have to apply to a Parole Board, who will then grant release only if they feel the prisoner is 'safe' to be released and rejoin the outside world.

Originally the sentence was intended for a maximum of 900 prisoners who had committed a very violent crime or sexual offence, but at its height, more than 8,000 prisoners were sentenced on the scheme. It became apparent that they were being used too extensively, and at one time almost seven per cent of the prison population was made up of IPP prisoners, many of whom were given the sentence for lower-level crimes. IPP sentences were abolished in 2012, but those on them still have to serve them.

There are many prisoners still behind bars, unsure when they will be released, trapped indefinitely within the system. This 'never-ending' sentence can be a psychological torment, for both the prisoners and their families, with high levels of self-harm reported. Some IPP prisoners have even taken their own lives.

Kim explained that she had gone through a number of Parole Board reviews, but none had gone in her favour. She was originally imprisoned for assaulting a stranger with the intent to steal their handbag, but she had also threatened her with a syringe and bitten her finger, knowing she had previously been infected with hepatitis B and hepatitis C. She also admitted that she did not even have a needle for the syringe with her, but nevertheless the threat created so much fear for the victim that her sentence had to reflect that. She had been under the influence of crack cocaine and heroin at the time, and had pleaded guilty to the offence.

Kim admitted that she felt awful about what she had done, and was particularly ashamed that she had threatened the victim with a syringe.

'I would never have done that to anyone, it was just a threat,' she said. 'I knew I couldn't really have passed hepatitis on to her as she was wearing gloves and I didn't break her skin, but I basically put her in fear of her life for six months. I wish I could turn back the clock.' She sighed deeply.

The crime was horrible, but I sensed that Kim was profoundly damaged, and was struck by how expressive she was. And in a way how accepting she was of her situation.

She was 23 when she had committed the offence that landed her in prison indefinitely. She had been released from prison only a month prior to that for a similar offence, when she had attempted to rob a stranger for money to fund her drug habit.

She had pleaded guilty and the judge noted her young age and her childhood trauma and maltreatment, but despite that she received an IPP sentence.

'I hate myself for doing what I did,' she said, running her hands up her arms, which had criss-crosses of old scars where she had hurt herself.

Seeing me look at her scars, Kim told me that one of

the reasons she had not been granted parole was due to her self-harm.

'They're concerned that I'll go back on drugs and start to reoffend and self-harm again on the outside,' she explained.

'Have you struggled with self-harm for a long time?' I asked.

Silently, she stood up and lifted up her tracksuit top and dropped her jeans to reveal the most horrific self-harm scars I had ever seen. Every part of her flesh was criss-crossed with extensive scars, like a haphazard drawing of the Underground map on her body. Some were raised and purple. Others had a grey hue and others were faded with age; it was clear that she had been assaulting her own body for many, many years.

I gasped. I was speechless; I had never witnessed anything like this before.

'I finally stopped cutting my belly when I was told I was at risk of disembowelling myself,' she said, matter-of-factly.

I was so disturbed that someone was so deeply trauma-tised that they could drive a blade into their own flesh this way. It was also incomprehensible how damaged they must be. I wanted to understand what had caused her to hate herself so much to hurt herself in that way.

'What caused you to do this to yourself?' I asked as she sat down again.

'I was abused by my mum and then my stepdad. He went to prison for it when I was a nine.'

I listened silently as she started to tell me more about

herself, giving me a potted version of her life. By then, it was way past the time I would normally be heading off home to do battle with the M25, but there was nothing to rush home for as my husband David was away for a few days on a sailing trip. I wanted to learn more about Kim, who was clearly a bright and intelligent person whose life had gone totally off the rails.

'I never really stood a chance of having a "normal" life,' Kim said. 'The social services knew about me before I was even born.' Kim's mother, Shirley, was already dealing with allegations of poor parenting of her sister and brother, who were only a year old and two years old when she was born.

Shirley was a victim of domestic violence and had a history of depression. She had another daughter a year after Kim was born, meaning that within five years, she had had four children. She had tried to leave her abusive husband Brian many times, but kept coming back for the security of another wage packet and a roof over her head. But the stress and violence took its toll.

'Mum would just shout and scream at us all the time, and often ended up hitting us. I longed for her to love me,' she said. For a moment or two she fell quiet, deep in thought.

By the time Kim was two years old, a social worker had been allocated to see the family, as Kim was found with bruising above her eye and three finger marks on her cheek, where she had been slapped. It seems that everyone was hitting everyone else in her family.

'My dad was beating my mum up for beating us up

basically,' Kim told me. 'I can sort of recall it happening. I think my mum was beating us up from the age of two. The angry child part of me thinks that was sort of fair enough really, but the adult part of me doesn't. Violence just breeds violence. Dad should've taken us and left.

'They split when I was five, and we only saw Dad at weekends. I know Mum found it hard. She used to say that we were running riot around the place; that we were out of control. I was first placed in care when I was six. Mum said she needed a breather. She had a very short fuse.

She continued: 'So me and my younger sister went into care and my older brother and sister stayed with her until she was found unconscious on the floor by a health visitor. She was a compulsive liar, and she was always overdosing on her medication. After that, we were all put in care.'

From then on, Kim and her siblings were in and out of care on a regular basis, due to the repeated and regular referrals from all the different agencies involved. There were ongoing concerns that her mother continued smacking the children, and frequently failed to pick them up from school.

'Sometimes we stayed with Nan, sometimes with foster families, and sometimes with Mum,' she told me, stating the facts without much emotion, her face blank, her eyes completely devoid of expression.

This was the hand that Kim had been dealt, but she talked about it in such a way that it was almost as if she was talking about the life of a completely different person, not her own brutal childhood.

'I know Mum was depressed, and some days she made it so obvious that she hated us being at home. I remember nearly always being the last kid to be collected from school, and I often began to panic, thinking she was never going to turn up.

'When I was six, she even asked the teacher if we could walk home, because she couldn't be bothered to come and pick us up. We were too young to find our own way home, so she had to meet us, but she was always late.

She fidgeted constantly as she chatted, and kept looking around the tiny room we were sitting in as if someone was going to suddenly appear from nowhere. A couple of times she even leapt out of her chair and made me jump. She was getting me going in the end, and later told me that this behaviour was in part due to the ADHD she had recently been diagnosed with.

Kim's mum met a new partner, Connor, who had two kids of his own of similar ages, and he moved into the family home. But despite there being another adult in the house, life was no better.

'Connor used to hit us with a stick, and Mum even admitted to our social worker that she kept the stick in the house for when she needed to punish us. She would hit us whenever we were out of line, and give us an almighty whack with that or her slipper when she felt like it,' Kim said. 'We were in and out of care like yo-yos. We would stay for a few weeks with a family, then Mum would ask for us back, saying that we had parties to go to and she didn't want us to miss out. I mean, of all the things to worry about, it was the McDonald's parties that she cared about the most. It just doesn't make sense.'

I felt sad that Kim had been let down by so many people in her past. I started to feel quite choked, as she spoke so lucidly about the trauma she had experienced.

Eventually, Kim and her siblings were all put on the 'at-risk' register due to concerns around possible sexual abuse, though medical examinations at that time revealed no evidence to confirm it.

'I remember having loads of interviews, when they kept asking us over and over again if we'd been touched inappropriately,' Kim said. 'I always said no, though I now realise I was far too aware about sex and stuff like that for a six-year-old. I remember saying that I hated being with Mum and Connor. I really can't remember what happened now – it all feels like such a blur.'

'Did you go to school?' I asked.

'I loved school and did well with my reading and sums, but I was teased 'cos I was always grubby – my uniform was never washed properly, and my shoes didn't fit; they were always a size too small,' she explained.

'Mum continued to hit us, even though she was told not to by the social worker. She often told us we should, "Fuck off back to your dad." She would also try to make school punish us by saying we shouldn't be allowed to go swimming. School can't have agreed to this, though, because every Friday we still went swimming; it was the best day of the week. Someone would always find us a spare towel.'

'Did it stop? The abuse?'

'Of course not. I was taken to A&E with slap marks on my face, after being reported by school. She hit me all the time. One day she said she hit me 'cos she was sad that the dog had died.'

She looked down, dejectedly. 'I still remember that slap – it felt as if it actually lifted me off the ground! She hit me so hard, it was like I'd been whacked by something far harder than her hand.'

I winced as she said these words. How painful that slap must've been.

Kim was then placed again into foster care with her siblings, and finally into a residential care home in a new area, which also meant she had to go to a new school.

'I was only seven and that's when things started to get really bad. I hated being in that home,' she explained. 'It was around then that I thought about suicide for the first time. Maybe if I wasn't around it would be better for everyone? Mum always used to say that to me, and I began to think it must be true.'

I felt so wretched for Kim. For a seven-year-old to be made to feel like that?

'The first time I attempted to kill myself, I tried to jump out of a window in the children's home. I thought I was worthless and unlovable. In my head, I remember thinking: *You're a tramp. You're a pig. You're a cunt.* They pulled me back and I just sobbed and sobbed, saying I hated myself. I begged to go home but Mum blamed me for everything that was wrong in her life.'

Kim looked me in the eye and shrugged.

'After that, I blamed myself for all of Mum's problems. Everything was my fault and I just wanted to disappear.'

It was at this point that I could no longer stop the tears from welling up in my eyes, and I let them fall silently down my cheeks. I was so overcome by the horror of her story that I simply couldn't help it. Kim came over to me and hugged me.

'Please don't get upset,' she said. 'I'm used to it. I've had to come to terms with so much bad stuff in my life. I just appreciate you listening to me and caring enough to feel for me.'

I hugged her back and our bond was sealed.

'I'm so sorry for everything you've been through,' I whispered. My sadness for her was overwhelming.

She had committed a crime and was paying the price for it, but I was starting to understand that she had had far worse done to her. Like so many of the women I came to know in prison, she was also a victim.

When Kim was seven years old, she and her siblings were made wards of court for the remainder of their minority. This is a measure used to protect and safeguard a child's welfare, and means the High Court has the ultimate guardianship over a child's protection, even though day-to-day care will sometimes remain with the parents, an individual or the Local Authority. Any step in the child's life then requires the court to provide their consent. They had been in and out of children's homes, and Kim's mother was ruled out as a viable long-term carer for them.

'We went back one Christmas for a few days. She called the authorities afterwards saying it didn't go well and that she didn't care about us any more. We smashed all our toys up, but I remember that none of us wanted to leave her, despite everything. I couldn't understand why I couldn't go back to my mum's until I was 16; it didn't make sense.

'Back at the children's home I kept trying to jump out the windows. I was smoking and climbing onto the roof,' she told me. 'When they took us on days out, I would cause as much trouble as possible. I remember once climbing on the roof of a football stadium. I used to love climbing onto roofs; it would get everyone's attention immediately. I even made my brother set fire to my bed whilst the other kids were sleeping.'

By that point, Kim had been permanently excluded from school. At eight, she stated in an interview that she wanted to kill herself, picking up knives and drinking disinfectant. She also stated that her mum's partner Connor abused her and her siblings when their mother was at bingo, but she had been too scared to tell her mum for fear of a beating. Following investigation and medical examinations, these allegations were proven, and he was found guilty of digital penetration and forcing her to perform masturbation and oral sex on him. The abuse had occurred repeatedly, and at the age of nine, Kim had to attend court to give evidence against Connor, and he was found guilty and sentenced to six years' imprisonment.

'He was charged with rape and indecent assault on all four minors,' Kim told me.

'It was around then that I started cutting myself with glass. I'd seen other girls at the home do it. It gave me such a feeling of relief. I even used to wish I was disabled so I could get more attention, and I could be pushed round in a wheelchair. Once I also stabbed myself with a screwdriver. The staff would always help me clean the wounds I inflicted on myself and put bandages on them. I knew I shouldn't do it, but it was like I couldn't stop myself.'

Not long after, her father was given custody of the children and they were each awarded a five-figure sum to be held in trust until their eighteenth birthdays from the Criminal Injuries Compensation Scheme.

'That seemed like more money than I could ever imagine. It didn't seem real. It was like being given a million quid. After that, it was decided I should go back to mainstream school. Things were pretty good at Dad's.'

Kim started at a new school and sat a psychological assessment that said she was a delightful little girl and had shown exemplary behaviour, with above average potential in cognitive testing.

I could tell she was bright; it was so obvious from talking with her, yet it was also clear that she had never stood a chance.

Despite everything, Kim longed for her mum to love her, but she made their relationship almost impossible after marrying Connor whilst he was on leave from prison.

'Somehow that evil shit Connor managed to get his sentence reduced on appeal, so was released from prison after only four years, and Mum married him while he was out on temporary licence. After all that bastard had done to us. It made me feel sick.'

There was talk of Kim and her siblings and dad moving to start afresh in a new area on Connor's release.

'We were scared he would come back and hurt us,' Kim told me. 'I still loved my mum – I still wanted her to love me, but I never wanted to see him again.'

The family did move for a fresh start, but by the age of 13, the children were back in care again because her dad was not coping and said he needed 'respite'.

How could so many people have failed Kim and her siblings? I wondered.

'We had the dirtiest home on the estate, basically,' Kim said. 'We felt like we had to be loyal to Dad, so never told the social workers what was happening at home. But both me and Stacey were expelled from school. We'd been smoking, swearing at teachers, shouting across the classroom and fighting. We didn't go to our detentions. I was desperate to fit in with the other kids, so started smoking weed.'

Their dad was drunk, so failed to make the exclusion panel meetings. Despite the fact she had been a grade A student, when she was focused and had the right support,

Kim never made it back to school and started to slip further off the rails. At 15, she had a 35-year-old boyfriend called Mike and was drinking and smoking cannabis regularly. She had also been scratching her arms but refused counselling.

'By then I was in a residential unit but I would always just go and stay with my boyfriend. People kept telling me Mike was no good for me, but I wouldn't listen. They tried to tell me he was abusive and exploiting me, but I didn't want to know,' she said. 'I was surrounded by really anti-social role models and a criminal lifestyle and I thought it was okay. I was involved with burglaries and thefts from the moment we moved to that estate.'

She was aged 16 when she was first arrested for robbery, after trying to steal a handbag and assaulting the victim. She had eventually made off with £15, taken from the victim's purse, and there was a knife with her fingerprints on it found at the scene. Kim pleaded not guilty because she was scared of prison, but eventually accepted responsibility.

During her court appearance, she was seven months pregnant with her first child.

'My boyfriend and me, we were working on market stalls,' she said. 'I just wanted to get pregnant and get married. I really wanted to be different from Mum; the complete opposite. I longed to have my own family to love and to lead a normal, decent life. Stupidly, I thought Mike loved me.

'I needed to prove that I was different to her. That I was capable of loving my kids. But Mike started being violent towards me. The first thing he did when I told him I was pregnant was slam my head against a wall. I was 17 when Alfie was born. I really loved that little baby with all my heart. I did everything for him; changed his nappies, gave him baths, gave him lots of cuddles. But we had no money 'cos I wasn't eligible for benefits and Dad couldn't claim for me neither.'

Kim knew she had to work hard to keep her baby and assuage concerns over Alfie's care, so she complied with the demands of the local authority that she engage with a thirteen-week assessment in a residential mother and baby unit.

'I was really proud of myself for passing that,' she said. 'They judged me to be a good mum.'

Three months after the birth of Alfie, Kim was pregnant again and facing homelessness. Her relationship with Mike by that point was on and off, and becoming increasingly unstable, and so she spent most of her time staying with her older sister in a bedsit, although their relationship was fragile and punctuated by arguments.

She explained: 'I loved my son so much and I did my best for him and I realised that if I reported Mike, Alfie would most likely be taken away from me, so I just let him hit me. He always won. He was six foot two, so he towered over me.'

A month after her eighteenth birthday, Kim's second son Ryan was born, and she managed to secure temporary housing. She also went on to acquire more clothing stock to try to grow her market stall business when she received her pay out, but her problems soon started spiralling out of control when Mike became increasingly violent.

It was at this point that she started using heroin and cocaine to blot out the horror of her abusive life, and very quickly became addicted as drugs took over her life.

The writing was on the wall.

'To start with they did put things in place for me with Alfie and Ryan, but I was too bad on drugs by then. Looking back, I realise I prioritised my drugs over my kids. I'm so ashamed. I separated from Mike and my drug use got right out of control. I was a shit mum.'

By the age of 21, Kim was dependent on heroin, and became suicidal again after her children were taken into care and adopted. She was homeless and made three further suicide attempts, twice by taking an overdose of tranquillisers and once by throwing herself in front of a car.

'Basically, after they went, I could see no reason to live. I was an emotional vacuum and felt completely numb and lost and empty. I knew I couldn't put up a fight for my kids,' she said. 'There was nothing left.' She sat silently staring at her feet.

'How have you found life in prison? Have you made friends?'

'Yeah, loads. And I've had relationships with women whilst I've been here,' she said.

'I went through a phase of feeling so dirty after being abused by that bastard that I was obsessed with making sure I was clean, and used to scrub my fanny over and over again with a scouring pad,' she told me, and as she did so I could feel myself shudder at the thought of how painful that must have been.

But she carried on as if what she had just said was normal day-to-day stuff.

'I look back now and have to admit that I always fancied girls, but ran with boys,' she smiled. She had had one significant relationship with a woman called Jade in another prison before they were separated.

'I loved her very much, and had great memories of our time together,' she said. 'I do feel a bit bitter though that they said I was violent towards her. There was no violence at all. She had a fit one night and hit her head on the corner of the desk. I was in the room with her at the time, and I was trying to help her get back to bed when she came around. Simple as. I would never hurt her. I loved her.

'Unfortunately, the relationship fell apart after we was moved to different prisons,' she said. 'But I lost my parole because they just wouldn't believe I didn't hurt her. It was a piss-take!'

Kim had recently been involved with someone else, but told me that she ended it when the other woman started using spice on the wing on a regular basis.

'It was just too dodgy. If they thought I was at it as well, I'd have no chance of getting through my next parole hearing,' she told me. 'I'm just desperate to know there's an end in sight, and that one day I'll be free. One day, I can start to live my life.'

Over the time that I have come to know more about Kim, she has described how hopeless she feels about her future, as she has no idea when she will be released from prison. She described with tragic insight the almost impossible task of serving an IPP sentence.

'When you lose hope your behaviour gets less controllable,' she said.

IPP sentences were intended for very few people, but it seems as if they were used far too frequently, perhaps to avoid difficult decision-making, leaving prisoners with no idea of when they will be released.

'It's an endless cycle of suffocation, desperation and frustration. I watch others come in, serve their time and leave,' Kim told me. 'I feel so angry that there's no end in sight for me.'

IPP prisoners are regularly moved between prisons and wings, and often struggle to settle into any sort of regular, stable routine. The confusion adds to the strain, anxiety, depression and sense of hopelessness that so frequently accompanies an IPP sentence.

At particularly low times during her sentence, Kim has gone through phases of using illicit drugs on the wing, especially spice, just to get off her head, with the attitude that if she can achieve nothing by abiding by the rules she may as well 'Fuck them!' to quote her. 'Spice is a great bird killer. The world isn't real any more. Trouble is, I end up back in the block on basic and then the shit reality returns.'

I was confused. 'Bird killer?'

'Yeah, because it makes the time go quick. In Cockney rhyming slang, bird lime means time. It all goes by in a bit of a blur and kills the time and takes your mind to another place,' she said. 'Your problems just disappear. It's bliss, until reality returns with a bang.'

After each Parole Board meeting, prisoners have to wait a year before they can apply again, although the process can sometimes take much longer.

I feel like Kim has not been given a chance to make it on the outside. During my time in prisons, I have heard of far worse crimes receiving much lesser sentences, including manslaughter. I just couldn't think what staying in prison was achieving for her.

She needed help to build a life. The burden IPP sentences place on not just the prisoner but their families must be unimaginable.

A relentless cycle of hope and despair.

'Not long ago I was given a large box, with five fat bulging lever arch files in it. My solicitor gave them to me. They were the records of my life and all the reports from social services, forensic psychologists. Everyone that was ever involved with my care from before I was even born. That's how I know what happened to me before I was old enough to remember. My life in a box!' She became lost for a moment in her thoughts.

'It took me a while to find the courage to read them, and first off, I couldn't bear to read some bits, but one entry talked about my PTSD when I had flashbacks of a little girl being abused. The self-harm was to block it all out. It made me question my whole being. I hated myself. Most of my life I've felt hopeless and lost.

'I feel like I've been left to rot in jail. I need to get out of here and try to make some sort of life for myself.'

Finally, she looked at me with eyes that I now realised hid a lifetime of sorrow.

'Where's a place in the world for me? How do I move on with my life? I just have the clothes I stand up in. I've done my time.'

Chapter Eleven

'A short prison sentence may as
well be a life sentence'

Standing at the front of the cavernous church, I took a deep breath and tried to calm my nerves. I have always avoided speaking in public as the thought of speaking in front of large groups of people terrifies me, but I was determined to conquer my fears and get through it. Despite working in prisons for over fifteen years and not feeling nervous, the idea of standing up in front of a large audience and speaking made me feel petrified. It's a fear I have had all my life.

I had been invited to speak at an event called the Safe Homes Summit at St Martin- in-the-Fields in London, about the health impacts for women of being released from prison into homelessness. I see this happen to so many prisoners that it is an issue that I feel passionately about.

This event was designed to identify the next steps for improving accommodation outcomes for women leaving prison to resettle in London. The event hoped to build on the London Blueprint: a plan aiming to tackle the root cause of offending, prevent reoffending, and ensure women have the support they need when they leave prison. This shared aim also works towards ensuring that women leaving prison are resettled into safe and suitable accommodation. The summit brought together leaders from all the key agencies, with the aim of gathering learning and sharing research and good practice, and identifying how better joint working could ensure these aims are achieved.

Homelessness is a complex and multi-faceted issue but one I feel needs serious attention to resolve. I refuse to brush the issue under the carpet, and there are many people who feel as strongly as I do. I hope that collectively we can start to make a difference to women who do not have a home, and the vicious cycle so many female offenders and ex-offenders find themselves in. For many of these women, with no home and a lack of support, they are simply being set up to fail.

Currently, over fifty per cent of prisoners are released from Bronzefield into homelessness every year, and the rising number of short-term recalls into prison and a desperate shortage of housing means that many women who are released in the morning are unsure if they will have a bed to sleep in that night.

'I have been working as a GP in prisons now for fifteen years, and have been at Bronzefield since 2015,' I said. I swallowed, feeling my mouth go dry. 'For the past two years, I have mainly been working with substance misusers, and I find it absolutely horrifying that the majority of people I deal with are released into homelessness. It never stops shocking me, and I doubt it ever will.

'I am more surprised now if the women say they have a home to go to than if they don't, which I think is a tragic reflection of the times we live in.'

As I started talking, I felt my nerves settle a little. I continued: 'Very often when the prisoners stabilise from drug and alcohol withdrawal and are able to engage comfortably, they will talk of their hope to get off drugs and turn their lives around, so they can be reunited with their children and their families. But however well they may do in their attempts to detox while in custody, and however much they long for a better life, almost without fail they tell me if they are homeless on release, they will be back doing drugs again to enable them to cope, and to block off the horror of the reality they are living.

'Sometimes they say they will try and get shelter in a crack house, but entry to the crack house, I am told, requires drugs. Continued drug use usually leads to chaotic lives, often further crime with the risk of repeated imprisonment, and can also have devastating effects on their general health.

'Injecting drugs can result in deep, painful chronic skin ulceration, gangrene, amputation, sepsis, deep vein thrombosis, pulmonary embolism, HIV, hepatitis B and C, which left untreated may lead to cirrhosis and liver failure. Many women also suffer from heart disease as a result of drug use, and many are underweight, malnourished and have no teeth left.

'Anybody who saw these women every day, coming in and out of prison I am sure would feel as I do, that the situation has to change somehow. It is heartbreaking.'

I talked about the fact that a lot of women do not seek appropriate medical care and tell me that they do not have a doctor 'on the out'. Many of them, unfortunately, do not realise that they can register with a GP, even if they do not have a fixed address. I have read that the average age of death for a woman who is homeless is 43.

This is a shocking statistic.

'I have met so many women who were homeless when they arrived in prison, some having been homeless for many years, and who would almost certainly be homeless on release,' I continued

'Many women live in horrendous situations, often compounded by mental health issues, and have suffered, from appalling abuse, both in their childhoods and adult relationships. Sleeping on the street, as opposed to sofa-surfing, is the most desolate form of homelessness, and gender-specific services to address their needs are not easily accessible.

'So many times, I have shed tears with and for these women. I am unable to even imagine the horrific lives they have had to endure. I sometimes ask them how they cope, and one lady said she was sleeping in a bin chute outside a One Stop Shop so she could retrieve out-of-date food when it was thrown in the bins. Others said that they did not really know how they coped, and many said that they sleep during the day, sometimes in public lavatories, as they are too frightened to sleep at night for fear of being raped.

'There are many more stories – of women finding old bits of carpet to wrap themselves in, to huddle in stairwells.

Some tell me that they sleep on night buses, or on one of the five Tube lines that run all night on Fridays and Saturdays.

'Others sleep in recycling bins housing dry waste like plastic and cardboard, where it is warm, and no one can see them. One woman I met recently in prison told me that she sleeps in a lift, and another has made a home in a derelict warehouse in which she has pitched a tent. To get into the warehouse she has to crawl through a small window. There is no electricity, so she uses candles to light her way at night. That is how she survives.

'Their sentences are often far too short to achieve any form of rehabilitation – some have said that a short sentence may as well be a life sentence. The success stories mostly come from those in prison long enough to get off drugs to find themselves again, often then being able to engage with learning and training. However, at any one time, around a third of residents are locked up for three weeks or less and return repeatedly into prison, of course, with enormous cost implications,' I continued.

'I was lucky enough to visit a women's centre in Birmingham a few weeks ago, called Anawim – an old Aramaic word referring to the poor, lonely, outcast and downtrodden people. Those with no voice. It was inspirational and a beacon of hope, and if such a model of excellence could be replicated up and down the country the world would be a better place,' I said as I concluded my talk, nerves still on edge but hugely relieved to get through it, and to step down from the stage and find my seat.

*

I had been invited to visit Anawim by my dearest friend who runs an international and hugely successful business, and who has also been very involved with various charities for many years.

After hearing my stories about the countless homeless women I have met in prison, she was inspired to try to address the horror of homelessness. After researching on the internet, she stumbled across Anawim, and arranged a visit with me.

We were both blown away by the place.

The charity provides support services to women and children at the centre, as well as in the community. They offer a long list of services, including rehabilitation services, financial and debt advice, counselling, accommodation advice, one-to-one support from case workers, support on family issues, courses in academic subjects, arts and self-esteem, and early intervention to divert vulnerable women away from a life of crime. They also provide short-term accommodation, particularly for women leaving prison who have nowhere else to go. We were so impressed by the passion and dedication of the people that work there. It was beyond inspirational, and the women we met all had nothing but praise and deep gratitude for the help they had received, some going as far as to say that it had saved their lives. Figures show that it costs around £65,000 per year to keep a woman at Bronzefield. To me, the money would be far better spent providing community rehabilitation and specialist women's centres. The people gathered in the church were trying to find a solution to this crisis, and I feel that centres like these could provide one.

Many women become homeless because they lose their homes whilst they are in prison. If a woman lives in social housing and is imprisoned, she is likely to lose that home while away, even if the sentence is very short. What makes this harder is that local authorities can categorise someone who has gone to prison as that person making themselves homeless. The reasoning is: you committed a crime, you knew you'd go to prison, and knew you'd lose your home. Once someone is considered intentionally homeless the council is under no obligation to find them a home. Of course, a lack of appropriate and safe accommodation increases the risk of reoffending. I am aware of one woman who was in prison for theft and was subsequently released onto the streets, where she was arrested for anti-social behaviour for sleeping in a park, only to be later released homeless. For some women it is a never-ending cycle of spending time in prison, being released without a stable home, reoffending and then spending more time in prison.

Many women are desperate to find private accommodation, but rents and deposits make it hard for them to get settled. One woman I met at Bronzefield, called Carrie, had been homeless for many years. She was in her forties and told me how she tried to maintain her dignity by always managing to wash every day and look clean and tidy.

'Some people who live on the streets really let themselves go, understandably, but my morning routine used to be to go into a large supermarket, to the mother and baby changing room, to wash and condition my hair in the sink and dry it under the hand dryer. Then I would strip wash – sometimes even shave my legs – get dressed, put my make-up on, and then head off to the library to plug my phone in to charge. Whilst I was there, I would plug in my hair straighteners to do my hair.

'It is so important for me to try and maintain my dignity, the same as most other people. I like trying to look and feel good. Don't get me wrong though, there have been many times when I've been so desperate, I've walked along Clapham High Street, asking for spare change for food because I was so hungry. When I say that I'm homeless, I can tell that people look at me and think I look too neat and tidy to be homeless and they just pass me by. I don't look dishevelled and unkempt enough to fit their preconceptions.'

She spoke to me about the issues surrounding debt, and her inability to find affordable housing. Despite being in a stable relationship, she has still failed to pull herself from poverty.

'So, I end up shoplifting again, and then back in court, which makes me clock up more unpaid fines. I've literally sat for hours and hours scrolling the internet looking for a private rental, but unless you have £500–£1,000 deposit, plus one to two months' rent upfront, there's no hope.

'I don't want much. My partner and I, we just want a base and a place to call home. We just want somewhere with a bed and washing facilities that is just ours. I feel that life is against me and I don't know what to do,' she said looking downhearted. 'I don't want to be 50 and still be in this situation. I would live in a cupboard if I could find one.'

Without stable accommodation, it makes it almost impossible for women to access training opportunities or find employment, to arrange benefits, or to re-establish contact with their families and rebuild relationships. This makes them easy targets for traffickers.

Not long ago, I saw someone's name on the appointment ledger for my clinic and alongside the name was the comment: 'Do not remove. Only wants to see a female doctor', and at that time I was the only female doctor on offer.

When I saw her, she was very friendly and chatty and was keen to explain why she only wanted to see a female GP.

'I had an appointment last week but when I saw on my appointment slip that it was to see a male doctor I refused to attend. Michelle, the officer on the wing, said I was daft not to attend. She told me that it should make no difference at all, and that she was happy to see a male doctor as they are professional people etc. etc.

'She went on and on and on until finally it was getting on my nerves, and I had to stop her mid-sentence and asked: "Have you ever been raped?" It stopped her in her tracks, and she looked shocked and embarrassed and couldn't answer for a moment, and then said, "No, never, thank God."'

'Well I have and that's why I cannot cope with seeing a male doctor.'

*

Mirela was 24 and was homeless. She had addictions to crack and heroin when she was sentenced for four months for shoplifting. She had grown up in Romania, and over the time I saw her during our regular meetings to deal with her addictions, I got to know her better.

She was abandoned by her parents when she was six weeks old, and grew up in care, in a series of different children's homes, all of which she hated.

She had never known her parents or had a proper family life. She was a pretty girl, with short blonde hair, and spoke so quietly that I struggled to hear her.

When I first met her, she was unable to hold eye contact for more than a second or two, preferring to look at her feet, which she tapped nervously as we spoke.

'I never knew my parents; I don't know anything about them, or if I have brothers or sisters. I would so love to have a family to belong to,' she told me.

'I loved school. I was good at learning and languages. I spoke quite good English. But I never had a settled home and never trusted anyone.

'I was raped when I was 13 by a group of older boys. It was at the home I was staying in. It made me realise that I had to escape from that shithole of a home. One day, not long after, I met a man called Andrei.

'I was having a coffee in a small café just around the corner from the kid's home. He was there too. We got chatting.

'He was really friendly and said that he could help me start a new life in England. I believed him. I feel so stupid now.

'Before I knew it, he had arranged my ticket and travel documents and everything, and I was on my way.'

Mirela arrived in the UK with Andrei and he took her to his friend's house, which was on the outskirts of the city. She would spend the next seven years in enforced prostitution.

'We were at the door and he said to me, "Stay here with my friend. I will be back in a short while." I had no idea what was going on.'

That was the last time Mirela ever saw Andrei. As soon as she entered, the door was slammed behind her and a man pulled out a knife. That same night she was taken to a bedroom for her first client. An ugly old man with a bald head and tattoos was lying on the bed waiting for her. The first of many many more.

She explained: 'I was a prisoner. I had no idea where I was and the curtains were always shut. I hardly ever saw daylight. There were other girls. Most of them looked even younger than me. And new ones kept arriving; new girls, who looked younger and younger. I didn't trust anyone. I didn't know if the girls were friends with the men, so I kept myself to myself.'

Mirela was raped every day, repeatedly, by many men.

'They did things to me that I never have imagined were possible,' she told me. 'As the men came and went, so did my hope. If I refused to do what they asked, I'd be beaten. They told me that if I didn't do it, I would owe them more money. Money for shelter and the small amount of food they gave me. I tried to stop taking care of myself, so the men would not choose me, but it didn't work. They couldn't care less what I looked like. They just wanted sex with a kid.'

I felt horrified and sickened that there were men in the world who would treat a young girl like this. It made my stomach churn.

For many weeks at a time, Mirela would not be allowed out, and sometimes they would move location, where she would be bundled into a car and driven for miles; she had no idea where they were. Every location they went to was cramped. 'It stunk, always of sweat, cigarettes and alcohol,' she told me. 'The men would sit in the front room with their phones and laptops, setting up business for us. If I cried, they just laughed at me.'

The girls were often starved; on some days Mirela said she would survive on a piece of bread, or somebody else's leftovers. She was only allowed to sleep when there were no clients, so could be working for twenty hours a day.

Eventually, and perhaps inevitably, one day Mirela realised that she was pregnant. She had no idea how far into the pregnancy she was.

'They told me that once my baby was here, they would make me continue working,' she said. 'I knew then that I had to do everything I could to get out of there. I was so skinny and hungry all the time. I thought I might die, or the baby would die.'

She miscarried not long after this.

'I started to bleed really heavily and had the worst pain I had ever experienced. And that's saying something, after the brutal attacks and rapes I'd been through. I knew I'd lost the baby. I had no idea it could be so painful,' she told me.

I felt so sad for Mirela that she had to go through such a painful experience all alone.

'I knew I had to get away, somehow, anyhow.'

'How did you manage to escape?' I asked, eager to hear how she escaped the clutches of these awful men.

'I got out one night. They were all watching TV. I grabbed the few things that I had and threw them in a plastic carrier bag. I climbed out of a window and ran for my life,' she said, almost breathless as she relived the experience.

Mirela just said she ran and ran until she was too exhausted to go any further. Eventually, she hid in some woodlands by a main road until daylight.

The next day she hid in a ditch, looking out for large lorries in the distance. 'I knew the driver of a big lorry could not be any of the bastards that had locked me up. And after many hours, one stopped! I told him, "I don't care where you are going, I am begging you to take me as far from here as possible."

'I think he felt sorry for me – I was a mess. I have never been so scared in my life. I knew that if I did not get away, they would kill me.

'I will never ever forget that amazing man that gave me a lift that day. He saved my life.'

She smiled at the memory fondly.

'I am convinced that he was a guardian angel in disguise sent to save me. He was kind enough not to ask me anything; why I was running away or who from. He just waited for me to talk with him, when I wanted to and was ready to. He also had some sandwiches, crisps, chocolate, and two bottles of water. He insisted I have them.

'I was starving. I don't think food has ever tasted so good.'

Mirela eventually found herself in Kent but had no one to turn to for support or help.

'I found myself on the streets and the only way I could survive was by shoplifting. I also then started to take drugs, to block out what had happened to me. It is one of the biggest regrets of my life, but I don't know how I would have coped without them.'

Soon Mirela was addicted to heroin and crack, and sometimes resorted to sex work to get money to pay for drugs, as her habit got out of control.

'It was all I knew. I hated it, but I couldn't make enough money doing anything else. Most of the men I never had a problem with, but there were certain types of weirdo out there that wanted me to do stuff to them that I really hated. It made me feel sick.

'Some also beat me up. It was scary. I never knew what I was in for when they paid their money. But after a lifetime of abuse, I guess I had learned how to deal with it.

'Once or twice, a lonely old man just wanted to be with

a woman. He would take me to a café for something to eat and a chat. It was weird,' she shrugged. 'But it was nice. Sometimes other blokes would take me out for a drink and we'd end up doing drugs together. They didn't all want sex. But it was like I didn't know what it was like to ever be treated normally.

'I never trusted anyone, or believed anyone could ever like me for who I am, rather than what they could get from me. In the past, when a man hugged me, they were pinning me down to have sex.

'I had no friends. No one. Except my Aunty Tania.'

'Aunty?' I asked, slightly puzzled.

'Yes. My one friend. She is from Street Angels.'

These are volunteers who run soup kitchens and other mobile support units and cafés. They also patrol the local communities on busy nights to talk with homeless and vulnerable people.

'She came to find me every week for four years, and would give me food and help me get the support I needed. But I was so scared about being sent back to Romania. Or the bastards finding me. I saw their faces everywhere.

'When I came to prison it was such a relief to have a bed and feel safe at night, and also to get help with my addiction. I may also get a place in a hostel when I leave, if I am really lucky. I pray every night for a miracle as I know that is probably what it would take to get a roof over my head one day.'

I was reviewing Mirela in the clinic for a routine check-up.

She had been in prison for the past four months, and was stable on 30ml of methadone. Three days before I saw her, she had received the news that a place in a hostel had been found for her after her release from prison the following week. This would be the first time in her life that she would have her own room to sleep in at night, and not be afraid. But when I saw her, she was sweating and clutching her stomach in pain, as she had not taken her methadone for three days.

'I want to start afresh,' she cried. 'I've had enough of this life. I cannot believe I will finally have my own room for the first time. I haven't taken methadone since the day I heard the news.'

I was astonished. I had never heard her sounding so positive and hopeful, despite the fact that she was feeling so ill.

'It's incredible news, Mirela,' I said. 'You must be so excited! Most people come off methadone gradually. They don't just stop like that! No wonder you're feeling so dreadful.'

'Yeah, but I can get through this,' she said. 'It will be SO worth it. I finally have hope. I cannot tell you what this feels like. I am desperate to stop taking drugs. I don't want to be controlled by them any more. I have to be free of this when I get out. I feel scared but there are people who will help me. Tania is coming to meet me from the gate. She is going to help me.'

There are some remarkable and compassionate people on the outside and Tania was clearly one of them.

I prescribed medication to try to help her cope with the symptoms of withdrawal, but was worried that she may not cope with stopping her methadone so suddenly from 30ml.

She came back to see me two days later as she was feeling really unwell. She was accompanied by Tom, her recovery worker, who was very supportive and concerned about her.

We were all aware that she may still have cravings, and that if things were difficult for her after release, she might well be tempted to use heroin again.

Tom said: 'I just wonder if Mirela could go back on a small dose of methadone, so that at least when she's released she will be under the care of the community DIP team and can detox safely with their help and support, if that's what she wants to do. That way there will then be people to look after her when she's out.'

I agreed: 'I think that would be much safer for you, Mirela. Are you happy to do that?'

She looked downcast and dejected.

'Yeah. I feel so crap. I feel so disappointed, but if I feel this bad when I am out, I am really scared I will use again.'

She started to cry, and we all sat silently for a few moments as Tom passed her some paper towel to dry her tears.

'I'm sure it's all going to be fine, and I think Tom's plan makes a lot of sense,' I said eventually, breaking the silence. 'Don't see this as a failure.'

Mirela managed to dry her tears and smile a little. We agreed to keep her on a very small dose of methadone, so she could be under the care of the Drug Interventions team outside.

She told me that she had spoken to Tania on the phone the previous evening, and had sobbed down the phone to her, telling her about how anxious and scared she felt about being released, as she was terrified of failing and of getting back on to drugs.

'I told her that she couldn't possibly understand what I was going through, and asked her how she could ever imagine or begin to understand what it feels like to be addicted to drugs? To be so scared of failing, and to feel as vulnerable and as low as I was feeling.

'But I couldn't believe it when she said: "Mirela, I have been clean for twenty-one years. I do understand. I was homeless once."

'I had absolutely no idea that she had been homeless and addicted to heroin, too.

'In all the years I had known her she had never told me. I could not believe it.'

'Hearing that inspired me with hope. I know she is there for me, and that she does understand. With her in my life, I feel I might just make it. Maybe my life at long last will begin to make sense. Maybe I will one day be happy,' she said.

As she left, we shared a comforting hug.

'Good luck, Mirela,' I said, 'You are a strong and special person. Believe in yourself.'

Epilogue

'But for the Grace of God go I'

It was 8 a.m. on a freezing cold morning a few days before Christmas. Even in prison, a buzz of festive cheer was in the air.

A pretty Christmas tree stood in the Healthcare waiting room with a scattering of baubles and lights, while other festive decorations were on display along the corridor.

As I turned on the computer to start work, I wondered as usual what challenges and dramas the day might bring: Whose names would be on the list? How many repeat prescriptions would need to be sorted? What variety of human ailments and emotions would I encounter?

While the computer was loading, I filled the kettle for my usual large mug of coffee to enjoy with a Danish pastry, a real treat that I only allowed myself on work days.

Some of the names on the list were unknown to me but most were familiar, including three homeless women who had just returned to prison. They all told me that they had tried to get arrested so that they would not be spending Christmas on the streets, freezing and alone.

As I looked at the work that had appeared on the screen Nicola, one of the Healthcare Assistants, popped in with a big smile across her face.

'Hi, Doctor Brown. Happy Christmas,' she said. 'I've brought you in some mince pies. I made them yesterday, so I hope you like them. And guess what… Kim has been transferred to start her open conditions. Isn't that great?'

As she said that a strange feeling shot through me.

Kim had gone.

The chances were I would never see her again. I was delighted that she had progressed to open conditions, of course, but I was yet again reminded of the transitory relationships that are a fact of prison life and work, the unlikely friendships that are forged which wouldn't necessarily happen in the outside world.

People, often from totally opposite walks of life, sharing moments of connection that defy convention, which is one of the joys, but also part of the sadness for me, of working in prison.

I thought of the first time that I met Kim, over two and a half years ago, and of how deeply her story had affected me.

'Oh, Nicola, thank you so much for the pies. I do hope Kim will be okay. I'm just sorry that I never had a chance to say goodbye.'

'I'm sure she'll be fine,' she said softly, with a shared understanding.

'Enjoy the pies,' she replied with a big smile, as she went

off to finish all her other jobs before starting the clinic with me at 9 a.m.

I sat for a moment thinking about Kim, and hoped so much that she would eventually get her freedom and find happiness. She had waited long enough for it.

My thoughts were broken when Haj, one of the nurses from House Block Four, tapped on the door and popped in. I was deeply fond of Haj. We had worked alongside each other for years, and he was definitely up there with the best.

'Hi Doctor B. Kim asked me to give you this,' he said as he handed me a note written on the back of a blood test form.

The handwriting was beautiful, all straight lines and completely uniform.

It read:

Dear Amanda

Thank you so much for all your time, support, belief and patience! Without you, people like me would have nobody and nowhere to turn to.

Please stay in contact with me. I will write to you.

Please write to me and come and visit me. You're an amazing lady and to say I love you and owe you my life doesn't go far enough.

All my love, Kim.

It was like getting an early Christmas present.

I was really touched by her words and my mood changed

in a heartbeat and I felt instantly positive about the day ahead.

It is hard to adequately explain the variety of different friendships and relationships I have been lucky enough to experience over the past fifteen years that I have spent working in prisons, and the joy for me is that most of them are with people I would be very unlikely to meet in my day-to-day life if I had never worked in such an environment.

A totally fascinating mix of people, often with the most extraordinary stories to tell.

*

Just before finishing for the day I heard carols being sung, and I couldn't resist popping out of my room to find out where they were coming from.

I followed the sound to the Healthcare wing, where I found four Salvation Army officers singing their hearts out, while another was playing a trumpet.

It was really beautiful and surprisingly moving, especially when they played one of my favourite carols, 'In The Bleak Mid Winter', which I can hardly ever get through without welling up as it takes me back to childhood memories and thoughts of loved ones lost.

When the carol singers moved on to another part of the prison, I went back to my room to finish typing up my notes before finally logging off for the day.

As I set off for home, everyone wished each other a

Happy Christmas and I walked across the yard with a couple of officers to the Admin block.

After locking my keys in the cabinet, I pressed on the biometric to open the barrier, waited for the doors to slide open to let me into the airlock, and then out the other side when the first door slid shut and the second door slid open.

After a cheery wave to the officers in the gate house I was off to start the usual slog home on the M25.

On the way I found myself thinking about what it must be like to spend Christmas in prison. Some people were clearly relieved to be there, to shelter from the cold and have company and a hot meal, but most must be longing to be with their families. There would be the usual mix of prison and healthcare staff working too, so that life in the prison could function as normal, like any other day, but I hoped there would be some fun and laughter as well if possible.

For my part I was not due to work again until 27 December, so I could look forward to spending time with my precious family, but for some strange reason I suddenly felt overwhelmed with appreciation of my freedom.

Although I have been aware of how lucky I am many times since I started working in prisons, more than ever before I became acutely aware that anyone could end up in prison if their life took a wrong turn.

'But for the Grace of God go I,' echoed through my mind as I continued on my journey home.

Acknowledgements

I was very reluctant to attempt a second book, and initially when I was asked to write a follow up to *The Prison Doctor* I declined, as I felt that I had used up all my stories. One book was enough.

On reflection, however, I soon realised that almost every day when I am at work, I hear of something that touches me very deeply, and that I am in a position to bring these stories to a wider audience. In doing so, I hope that perhaps some good may come from raising awareness of the abuse so very many women in prison have suffered, and of the shocking and horrific ongoing issue of homelessness.

I learned within a very short space of time after starting to work at Bronzefield, that so often the crimes the women had committed were the result of the unimaginable lives and suffering they have had to endure, and so despite my reluctance and anxiety I agreed to attempt a second book.

For this I owe my thanks to Susan Smith for her encouragement to embark on book number two, and for her ongoing support and friendship.

Also, to my editors, Kate Fox for all her help, guidance,

and passion for the subject matter, and to Nira Begum and Jamie Groves for their invaluable contribution.

Thanks also to Joe Thomas at HQ who helped give me the courage to face all the publicity involved with the first book. As a naturally shy person it was an ordeal I don't think I could have got through without him by my side.

My deepest gratitude goes to Georgina Rodgers for helping me to write this book and with whom I have shared so much over the past six months. Thank you for listening to me and allowing me to literally cry on your shoulder at times. Thank you too for all the laughter. I am so grateful to you for all your hard work and for pushing me on when I was slowing down. I hope our friendship will continue to flourish.

Thanks to all the staff at Bronzefield, for their co-operation and all the wonderful work they do, and to all the residents who have trusted me with their stories.

On a personal note, as always, my thanks go to my wonderful husband David, the love of my life, my rock, and my soul mate. Thank you for putting up with the emotional wreck I am at times when I get home from work, and for always managing to make me laugh.

My love too as ever to my beloved sons Rob and Charlie, my beautiful daughter-in-law Claire, and my dearest sister Laurie. You make my life worthwhile, and the love I have for you all is beyond words. I feel so blessed to have you in my life.

To my delight, my dearest friend Vanessa is still by my

side, listening to the stories that affect me so deeply, and comforting me when sadness overwhelms me. Thank you for your immense compassion and generosity which has made a difference to more lives than you will ever know, including mine.

Lastly, I am really grateful to everyone who wrote to me after the first book, and to those who were kind enough to write positive comments about it.

Thanks to you too, for choosing to read this book.